# GOOD WITH ME

*Praise for*

# GOOD WITH ME

"Patricia's new book gives us many thoughtful and attainable ways to step out of our unexamined ways of thinking and living that lead to discontent. Her philosophy and methods take us deeper into knowing ourselves and what we truly want in life. All who study this book will grow into more of who they want to be."

**—Jacquelyn Small**
Author of *Awakening in Time and Becoming A Practical Mystic*

"If you have ever reached a goal and yet not felt satisfied, reading this book will show you why that is and how you can change that. Permanently."
**—Laura Atchison**, Business strategist, international speaker, and bestselling author of *What Would a Wise Woman Do?*

"As an image consultant to the stars, I value Patricia Noll's *Good With Me* because it acknowledges that it isn't enough to be famous, impressively dressed, and perfectly coiffed to enjoy the lasting good feeling about oneself for real. The good feelings that come from outer beauty are short lived, while the good feelings that come from the inner knowing that we have value and are beautiful just because we exist is key to real happiness from the inside out."

**—Starley Murray**, Celebrity image expert, brand expert, publicity strategist, and media trainer

# GOOD
## WITH ME

A Simple Approach to Real Happiness
from the Inside Out

## PATRICIA NOLL

New York

# GOOD WITH ME
## A Simple Approach to Real Happiness from the Inside Out

Published in New York, New York, by Morgan James Publishing. Morgan James and The Entrepreneurial Publisher are trademarks of Morgan James, LLC.
www.MorganJamesPublishing.com

The Morgan James Speakers Group can bring authors to your live event. For more information or to book an event visit The Morgan James Speakers Group at www.TheMorganJamesSpeakersGroup.com.

A **free** eBook edition is available with the purchase of this print book.

ISBN 978-1-61448-746-3 paperback
ISBN 978-1-61448-747-0 eBook
ISBN 978-1-61448-748-7 audio
ISBN 978-1-61448-873-6 hardcover
Library of Congress Control Number:
2013945999

CLEARLY PRINT YOUR NAME ABOVE IN UPPER CASE

**Instructions to claim your free eBook edition:**
1. Download the BitLit app for Android or iOS
2. Write your name in **UPPER CASE** on the line
3. Use the BitLit app to submit a photo
4. Download your eBook to any device

**Cover Design by:**
Rachel Lopez
www.r2cdesign.com

**Interior Design by:**
Bonnie Bushman
bonnie@caboodlegraphics.com

In an effort to support local communities, raise awareness and funds, Morgan James Publishing donates a percentage of all book sales for the life of each book to Habitat for Humanity Peninsula and Greater Williamsburg.

Get involved today, visit
www.MorganJamesBuilds.com

Habitat
for Humanity®
Peninsula and
Greater Williamsburg
Building Partner

*What I am feeling now,*
*Is exactly what I choose to be feeling.*
*I know that everything in my life*
*Has brought me to this moment in time,*
*And I am exactly where I choose to be*
*Perfect in my imperfection,*
*And thereby human.*

Patricia Noll, founder of Focus One, Inc.

*For my friend and mentor, Dr. Livingston Otis,*
*who generously shared his wisdom with me and believed that*
*I could be who I am today before I could even imagine it*
*for myself. You left this life all too soon.*

*For everyone with whom I have had the privilege to share*
*any part of my life's journey. Each one of you has made a*
*contribution to me, and I am grateful that our paths crossed.*

*For my children, Diana and Tom,*
*who support me with unconditional love.*

*For Daisy, who lovingly kept me company*
*hour after endless hour as I wrote* Good With Me.

*For God, who gave me this gift to share with the world.*

# Contents

# On a Personal Note

I believe the key to real happiness exists within every one of us. I believe this is true because if someone like me can make the shift from extreme unhappiness to real happiness, you can too. I have been where you are: unhappy with me, discontent with life, angry, depressed, anxious, and addicted to just about everything on the planet. I was worried about my appearance and the way others saw me. I was a yes-person because I wanted to be liked. I was tired of working so hard to please others just to prove that I was good enough. What I share with you in the pages that follow is the result of my own life's journey and personal quest for real happiness, not the fake and phony kind of happiness I once experienced. I am deeply grateful to have the opportunity to share it with you.

To realize the promise of this book in your life you must commit to completing the *Exploration and Discovery* assignments in each chapter. That is the only way to achieve positive results. If you choose to skip over them, nothing much will change for you. Making the initial shift from unhappiness to real happiness demands a lot of energy. It necessitates conscious focus to accomplish surefire results. Compare this energy requirement to the enormous amount of energy needed to manage the chaos, crises, and stresses of your unhappiness.

I am absolutely convinced that the time has never been more right for each of us to learn how to experience real happiness from the inside out by becoming a Good With Me™ person. Let me explain what it means to be Good With Me. Good With Me people have transcended their search for someone or something to make them happy because they experience real happiness from within. They no longer envy those who have what they want. They no longer spend enormous amounts of energy and money to get approval from others. Instead, they are comfortable in their own skin. They approach the world around them in a relaxed and peaceful way. They approach life and others from a place of kindness, caring, and service. Their lives have taken on a higher purpose.

On an elementary level Good With Me people like themselves no matter who they are, what they have, what they achieve, or what others think about them. Good With Me people like themselves just because they exist. It's very simple. When people like who they are and believe they have basic fundamental value "just because," their unhappiness, discontent, depression, anger, rage, and violence dissipates. This is sorely needed at this time in our society because it provides a solution to some of our most challenging global issues.

As an author, speaker, consultant, licensed mental health counselor, certified addictions professional, acupuncture physician, and founder and owner of a state-licensed outpatient substance abuse program, Focus One™, I have spent more than twenty-five years treating thousands of troubled individuals from all walks of life (socioeconomic, educational, gender, sexual orientation, race, and culture). Many of these individuals were referred to me as the result of a drug- and/or alcohol-related offense. Others came to me voluntarily because their lives were falling apart. They were depressed, angry, anxious, unhappy, discontent, their relationships were a mess, they were in the middle of a nasty divorce, they were in financial trouble, and/or they had an addiction to someone or something, such as alcohol, drugs, food, shopping, gambling, sex, pornography, sexting, a particular person, television, Facebook, even their mobile phone apps and just about anything else you could possibly think of. I have become an expert at showing them how to make the shift from being *other-dependent* for their happiness to becoming *self-dependent* to experience real happiness from the inside out.

Let me give you an example of what I mean with the following client testimonial.

I just walked through the door behind you just like you did. I'm at Focus One. I don't know what to think. My life is a mess, unmanageable. My thoughts are *another hurdle to get my [driver's] license back, same old paperwork to fill out, same questions, still apprehensive but open-minded.* A few days later my first counseling session starts. I realize it's different than others. So I start to listen to Dr. Noll and the others in class. Slowly teachings sink in my mind and I'm amazed; low self-esteem that's me, the power of positive thinking and high self-esteem. *Can I do this?* It didn't take long to realize I could if I opened my mind's thoughts. Like a sponge I took it all in. I'm amazed. I thought I knew how to live life "wrong." I've just begun. We talk, we laugh, we learn. I turn my power and will over to God and start to control my thoughts. Almost immediately positive things start to happen. My third DUI is reduced to reckless driving, my license will be reinstated, my job as a firefighter is secure again. I'm amazed I'm exactly where I'm supposed to be. I've enjoyed my experience and now look forward to walking through that door. I encourage you to do the same. Soon I will head back to that door. I'm no longer apprehensive or worried, but happy, sad, and glad because now I can control my life and my thoughts because of Focus One, AA, and the people in my group who have taught me that I am who I am, perfect in my imperfections and special in my own way. So take from what's inside that door as I have. Higher self-esteem, the power of positive thoughts, and a way of life that God and our conscious minds will for us. It's funny as I head for that door. It's now open and won't close. It's a pathway now. As I pass through it into this universe it's a lot

*continued...*

*...continued from previous page*
brighter outside and I feel that I can accomplish anything. The possibilities are endless. I know now that door was just a door and I was meant to open it and walk through. Thank you, Dr. Noll, Jeff, Cory, Eric, and the rest of my group. By the way you might want to leave your old stuff inside. I did.
Sincerely, firefighter/EMT Paul Taylor

I have been privileged to interact with each and every person who has come to me for help no matter whether voluntarily or involuntarily. I have been equally blessed with the best teachers and mentors along the way and the support of caring and loving people in my personal life who have led me to the discovery of how to be a Good With Me person. I am grateful to be someone who enjoys real happiness that can only come from within. It is an authentic happiness and not the kind I used to pretend I had in order to look good to others so they would approve of me. It is a real happiness that anyone who is *self*-dependent can own and experience.

Because the time is right to share with you and the world how to become a Good With Me person, I am introducing my discovery and a step-by-step guide to real happiness in the pages that follow. Allow me to take you by the hand and share with you what I have learned and others have learned: how to be a Good With Me person. I am deeply honored to have the opportunity to do so.

Please know that I am still a student of the universe. I continue to learn each and every day just as you do. What I share with you here in these pages is the result of my own personal quest for real happiness. For me, learning how to become *self-dependent* so that I take responsibility for my own happiness is groundbreaking, exciting, and opens up unlimited possibilities that people like you and me could only dream about.

While I am happy to share what I have learned, please do not hesitate to seek professional help beyond this book. Neither I nor my publisher is responsible for the results you experience from the information presented in this book—either good or bad. As you will learn, it is you who are responsible for your own happiness. With that in mind, take responsibility as you go forward for becoming the best Good With Me person you can be, one who is self-dependent and enjoys real happiness from the inside out.

My intent for writing *Good With Me: A Simple Approach to Real Happiness from the Inside Out* is to start a Good With Me movement throughout our society.

I'd love to hear from you! Contact me at <u>www.goodwithme.com/</u> <u>movement</u> to become involved in the Good With Me movement, for corporate sponsorships, school programs, speaking engagements, and personal consultations.

XOXOXO,

Patricia

# Acknowledgments

In keeping with the promise of this book, as someone who is Good With Me, I acknowledge myself for persevering to present a simple solution to some of our challenging global issues.

I acknowledge every single person who has touched my life, from birth to present, whether a little or a lot, whether kindly or with animosity, whether with love or with hatred. Each one has made a major contribution to my life's journey that has led me from my other-dependent esteem to finally being Good With Me. Each one was a catalyst to my quest in life to find out why I was so unhappy most of the time while everyone else seemed to be happy.

My best friend, Dr. Livingston Otis, was the first to provide some real answers to my struggles with my unhappy self. I will be forever grateful for his wisdom and his unselfish willingness to share it with me. I am blessed that he believed in my ability to do the work I do today and for giving me a gentle nudge to pursue it.

Thank you, Lisa, for the invitation to Author 101. And thank you, Rick Frishman, publisher of Morgan James Publishing, for making Author 101 and the myriad of professionals available to me. The experience was life changing.

I am forever grateful for the wisdom of Laura Atchison, chief questioner, speaker, and bestselling author of *What Would a Wise Woman Do*. She immediately saw the WOW factor of my message and introduced me to Terry Whalin, acquisitions editor for Morgan James Publishing, who said, "Let's make it happen." Thank you, Terry. We did it. You and Laura will always have a special place in my heart.

My gratitude is enormous for David Hancock, founder of Morgan James Publishing. He interacts with me as though I am the only author he is ever going to publish. What a gift he shares with others. I am grateful to Lyza Poulin, my managing editor, for always having the answer. Lyza, you are great. My goal is to respond to all of my emails as quickly as you have always responded to mine. And finally I am grateful for all of my Morgan James team: Rick Frishman, publisher; Cindy Sauer, VP of operations; Margo Toulouse, managing editor; Bethany Marshall, marketing liaison; Nickcole Watkins, marketing liaison; Jim Howard, publishing director; and Kim Spano, author relations manager.

Amanda Rooker is an editor extraordinaire. She believed in the concept of *Good With Me* from the first manuscript review and would not allow publishing deadlines to trump the quality of the book's message. You have been a real gift.

My attorney, Peter Hoppenfeld, took excellent care of me. Hobie Hobart of Dunn Associates unselfishly shared his incredible knowledge about book covers, marketing, branding, and much more with me, the novice who knew nothing about book publishing. Jill Lublin, three-time bestselling author, publicity and networking expert, and international speaker, taught me the importance of publicity.

As a mentee of Tom Antion's remarkable Great Internet Marketing Training Program, I continue to receive everything I need to know and more through Tom and his knowledgeable and always helpful staff in order to create professional websites that work, learn the value of social media, master the art of great professional speaking, and the list goes on and on. Thank you, Tom. You are the real deal.

My brilliant shining star handler, Starley Murray, brand expert, publicity strategist, media trainer, and image expert—along with her team, Paty and Christine—has continuously been over-the-top miraculous. I love you all.

I have always been blessed with the best teachers in my journey. I am most grateful for every one of them.

I am full of gratitude for everyone who believes in the value of *Good With Me*, for everyone who has been waiting for it to be published, for everyone who keeps asking if it's out yet, and for the support of so many remarkable individuals along the way. A special thank you to Debra, Wendy, Carol, Mandy, Bobby, Julie, Steve, George, and Ellen for your support and for believing in the message of Good With Me.

I want my daughter, Diana, to know how much she is loved. I will always cherish her unconditional love and never-ending support during the times when I grew weary from the long hours of writing and revising a manuscript. And to my son, Tom, you are the best.

And finally I am grateful to God and the universe for the knowledge I have been given to share with the world.

# Introduction

Every generation throughout the history of civilization has had its own idea of what it means to be happy. And even though the definition of happiness changes from time to time, generation after generation has searched for that which by their own definition would make them happy. Likewise every generation has experienced the fleeting effect of whatever they depended upon for their happiness. Some thought it was just plain luck if you achieved it and others thought real happiness was too hard to attain. Thus the definition of happiness changed to accommodate those who sought it.

Today we have largely determined that happiness is dependent upon the accumulation of wealth and material possessions, achieving success by society's current standards, and plenty of approval from others. If this doesn't resonate for you, just think about how important it is to be "liked" on Facebook these days.

Our happiness has become completely dependent upon people and things outside of ourselves. In other words, our happiness has become *other-dependent*. If material possessions, accomplishments, and approval from others are in fact the basis for real happiness, why are the happy feelings so temporary when we have them? Why are so many still so unhappy? Why do we keep looking for someone or something else to make us happy?

Because we've been taught that whatever it is that will make us happy is out there somewhere. And if this is true, what chance does the person who lacks money, education, accomplishments, and approval from others have for being happy? Can they never have even a little bit of happiness? Are they doomed to be unhappy for a lifetime? Are they lost forever? Is that why so many are angry? Is that why so many have given up completely? Is it time to change the basis for happiness in this generation?

My original intent was to write a book strictly about recovering from an alcohol or drug addiction. Initially I agreed with the disease theory that argues that addiction is an illness that afflicts certain individuals. I soon discovered that treating the so-called addictive behaviors in the conventional sense, using the techniques I had been taught in and out of school, very seldom worked. Even when the techniques seemed to work, they didn't work for very long. Individuals kept relapsing.

I began to recognize that the use of alcohol and drugs and all other addictive behaviors—including food, gambling, shopping, relationships, sexting, pornography, Facebook, video games, mobile phone apps, and anything else—ran much deeper and was more complex than a disease theory. I finally recognized that putting someone into treatment or rehab to learn abstinence or how to "just say no" didn't fix anything. It only created a revolving door that just kept turning and turning.

A common thread revealed itself among my clients: a lack of self-esteem. No one felt good about themselves "just because." I began to question why this was so prevalent among almost everyone who came to me for help, no matter what the reason. This lack of self-esteem prompted me to look deeper into my own quest for happiness. It was during this exploration that I discovered *other-dependency*. I recognized that most of us have been taught to be other-dependent for our happiness and that society unknowingly promotes other-dependent esteem instead of self-dependent esteem. I was seeing firsthand how being other-dependent is responsible for the majority of our poor choices and addictive behaviors, and I clearly understood for the first time why traditional forms of treatment don't work very well.

If you or someone you know haven't experienced treatment or rehab, all you have to do is turn on the television to hear about the latest celebrity or politician to go into an expensive rehabilitation program. Then later on you hear about that same well-known personality going back again and again. This kind of rehabilitation doesn't seem to have much to do with long-term success. How could it when the focus of treatment is on a symptom of the real problem and not on the real problem itself?

Our other-dependent society has created a global challenge. According to current research, lack of self-esteem is at an all-time high, addiction to drugs and alcohol is epidemic, and individuals are experiencing more stress than at any other time in history.

I noticed that some individuals pretended to be happy, some pretended to have self-esteem, some even insisted they had it when it was obvious they did not, and others had given up hope of ever having either one. This led me to the discovery of what I call The Four Attachments™, which are (1) the need for approval from others, (2) the need to look good, (3) the need to be right, and (4) the need to control the way things work out. They exist because of the need for approval from others. They are the direct result of other-dependency and the global challenge our society is facing.

Applying what I learned to myself first and then my clients, I developed a unique treatment. I focused on the dynamic relationship between thinking, the role of *self-dependent* esteem versus the role of *other-dependent* esteem, the Four Attachments, and their influence on real happiness from the inside out.

*Good With Me* identifies and addresses the real problem: other-dependency. And it provides a blueprint for improving your life and reaching your highest level of potential.

To attain real happiness from the inside out while living in an other-dependent society, it is important to understand the difference between *other-dependent happiness* and *self-dependent happiness*.

Likewise it is important to understand how other-dependency fosters other-dependent esteem. It has mistakenly been thought that an individual has either high or low *self*-esteem. Not so. It is *other*-dependent esteem that varies from low to high because it is dependent upon changeable external sources. It varies depending upon, and not limited to, how much you are liked by others, being recognized for doing a good job, getting the promotion, winning the competition, wearing designer labels, living in the right house in the right neighborhood, and much more.

Since not everyone is a world leader, billionaire, celebrity, famous athlete, or favored politician, for some being liked by others depends upon being the meanest member of the gang, being feared by others, drinking others under the table, or getting high faster.

In contrast, *self-dependent* esteem is stable because it is not dependent upon external sources of any kind. Having self-dependent esteem means you esteem yourself from the inside out. It means you like yourself just because and for no other reason. Once you are a Good With Me person, it seldom varies!

So what does it mean to be other-dependent instead of self-dependent? I am a good example of what it means. I, like almost everyone else, have relied upon someone **and** something outside of myself to make me happy. I thought that being a good little girl would make my parents love me more. It didn't. I thought that making good grades in school would do it. It didn't. I thought that having the right friends would make others like me better. It didn't. I thought that playing sports would make me fit in and belong. It didn't. I thought that sitting first chair in the high school band would make me special. It didn't. I thought that having the popular boyfriend would make me popular. It didn't. I thought that marrying into the right family would make me happy. It didn't. I thought that having children would give me what I was missing. It didn't. I thought that having a career position that every man in the company envied would make me feel confident. It didn't. I thought that being a business owner would make me feel worthy. It didn't. I thought that having lots of money, a big house, an expensive car, and designer clothes would make me feel like I was as good as everyone else. It didn't. I thought that drinking alcohol would make me feel better. It didn't.

Nothing seemed to give me what I needed because I didn't know what I needed. I just wanted to be happy. What was wrong with me? I didn't know at the time that I was dependent upon someone or something outside of myself to make me feel good—to make me happy. When I stopped using alcohol to mask my unhappiness and lack of self-confidence, I had two choices. I could be doomed to a life of unhappiness or I could begin a quest to find out what was missing and how to fix it.

*Good With Me* is the result of my own personal quest. I have written this book to show others how to feel good about themselves and experience real happiness from the inside out. It's possible to enjoy self-dependent esteem without depending upon someone or something outside of yourself to do so. I want to share with others how to transcend their current limitations so that they too can become part of the solution to the global challenge of other-dependency.

While my theory of other-dependent esteem versus self-dependent esteem defies much of traditional psychology, it explains why so few people are ever truly happy from the inside out. It also explains why feeling happy for most is similar to a roller coaster ride—up and down and up and down. It comes and goes and comes and goes. It explains why so many individuals have given up on life and why anger, rage, and violence are so prevalent in the world.

*Good With Me* provides a simple approach to feeling good and being truly happy that lasts for more than a few minutes, hours, or days. It shows you how to change your thinking from negative to positive, how to let go of the ideas you were taught by an other-dependent society about who you should be, what you should be, what you should achieve, and what you should have in order to be happy. It shows you how to stop depending upon someone or something outside of yourself to make you happy. It shows you how to achieve happiness that belongs to you because it comes from the inside out instead of from the outside in.

People who have self-dependent esteem can make a mistake and not feel bad about who they are. They can make a poor choice without beating up on themselves (although the person with self-dependent esteem makes fewer poor choices because they are not always trying to second-guess themselves and make choices dependent upon getting approval from others). Yes, they might be disappointed that they made a mistake or poor choice or didn't win the gold medal, but they don't esteem themselves any less because of it. They still esteem who they are. They know they always have value and their value isn't dependent upon someone or something outside of themselves.

People who have self-dependent esteem remain happy even when they haven't accomplished what they should have accomplished by now, even when they are broke, and even when no one likes them on Facebook today. They don't have to fall apart emotionally to show others they care or feel deeply about someone or something. They don't stress over how to be liked and approved of by everyone they meet. They have overcome the Four Attachments, and none of that matters anymore.

Even if, at this very moment, you are completely dependent upon external sources for any bit of happiness you experience, the good news is that your brain is not hard-wired. Neuroscience has proven that our brains have plasticity and that when we change the way we think we create a new default on our own internal computer, the brain. A Good With Me life is attained by consciously monitoring our thinking and changing it from negative to positive to overcome other-dependent esteem and shift it to self-dependent esteem.

My mission is to make a difference in the way people value themselves through *Good With Me,* the Good With Me interactive website, social media, e-zines, e-courses, speaking engagements, and the media. Those who engage in this process will learn how to "positive-up™", to experience "what a difference a thought makes™", and how to experience real happiness from the inside out with self-dependent esteem. You will learn how to reprogram yourself to shift from other-dependent esteem to self-dependent esteem and finally experience real authentic happiness.

I have received thousands of client testimonials sharing the transformational results in their lives from practicing what is revealed in the pages that follow. Here is just one of those testimonials:

Dr. Noll is the most engaging, authentic, and inspirational mental health counselor I know. I have struggled with alcohol and depression issues since high school. I was on multiple medications for depression and sleep issues. After going through multiple stints in detox and rehab centers, I went to her with an open mind. My expectations were not high as I have been through different programs with the same results.

*continued...*

*...continued from previous page*

Our first one-on-one meeting was different than any other that I have ever encountered. We focused on my self-esteem not alcohol, what others thought of me, and relationship problems. I noticed a change in my approach and thinking to the daily issues that arise in our lives. The focus groups facilitated by Dr. Noll are intense. They take off the layers of problems by getting to the root of all of our issues in a group setting. Relapse was not an option.

It has been over five months since I first met with Dr. Noll. After going to weekly group sessions and monthly one-on-one sessions, I have a whole different outlook on life. I just don't go through the day on autopilot. I am aware of how my thinking affects everything in my life. I have been able to sleep without the help of medication. I don't have the want or need for alcohol to make me feel better.

Dr. Noll has a gift to truly listen and ask the questions that help you unlock your full potential. She is a leader in her field. In addition, she is a woman with a pure heart that has a deep passion for people and making our world a better place. Don't hesitate to work with her in any capacity. She's a "gem."

From the bottom of my heart, thank you Dr. Noll for all you have done to improve my quality of life.

Sincerely,

Nick Terzick

I look forward to hearing from you one day soon at www.goodwithme.com/resources.

My desire is that you too will learn how to reprogram yourself to shift from other-dependent esteem to self-dependent esteem and finally experience real authentic happiness.

Let's get started!

## CHAPTER ONE

# So You Want to Be Happy

Y ou *do* want to feel good, right? You're not alone. I seriously doubt there is anyone on the planet who doesn't want to experience happiness. With that in mind, *Good With Me* is not just another book to read and put on a shelf to be dusted off every now and then. It is a guide for living to be used every day and to be experienced for a lifetime. Why? Because this book will provide real answers to real-life issues that real people experience in their quest for the good life.

With that in mind, what will you gain from this book that you haven't already found in all the rest? Why bother reading another self-help book or attending another self-help seminar when you always end up in the same old familiar place after you leave the pages of the book or weekend retreat? Why bother when nothing changes—at least not long-term?

The reason to bother reading this book is because it is different from all the rest. It defies many concepts of traditional psychology. It might be compared to learning a foreign language. You may think you are walking around freely in life, but many of you will discover that you are actually trapped in a box. This box has a name: *other-dependency*. The confusing thing is that most of us call this box "self-esteem" and even "high self-esteem." But it is a box just the same.

Every single person who wants to feel good by achieving real happiness, no matter what, can do so! But let's be honest. Most of us were not taught how to make ourselves feel good. We weren't taught how to make ourselves feel happy either. In fact, we have been taught just the opposite. We were taught by our parents, grandparents, older siblings, aunts and uncles, schoolteachers, religious leaders, advertising media, social media, and just about anyone else we can think of to expect that someone or something outside of ourselves would make us happy. We were taught to be *other-dependent.* That's why most of us depend upon someone or something outside of ourselves to make us feel good. And you know as well as I that this kind of other-dependency doesn't work. Having other-dependent esteem is the root of unhappiness, discontent, addiction, anger, rage, violence, and even criminal behavior and suicide. It's a box we must free ourselves from if we truly want to be happy.

For example, were you one of those babies who walked earlier than your mom's best friend's baby? Did you know your ABCs before you began preschool? Did you know how to write cursive in kindergarten? Could you read better than the rest of the class? Were you the best in academics or athletics? Were you popular at recess? Did you wear the right tennis shoes or blue jeans? Did you graduate with honors? Why was any of this important? What message did it give us about how we should be? Are you beginning to get the picture? Are you starting to see how we have been taught to be other-dependent and to worry about what others think of us? How many people do you know who are worried about what others think of them? How many people do you know who are waiting for just the right someone or something to make them happy? Are you one of them?

Even though we haven't all had the same expectations to live up to and we don't all depend upon the same person or thing to make us feel good, the end result is always the same. It doesn't work! And even when someone or something does seem to make us happy, the happiness is only temporary. The happiness doesn't last so we have to look for someone or something else to make us happy all over again.

So who was this book written for? I wrote it for everyone who wants to be happy and doesn't know how, no matter your age, race, or skin color.

No matter where you live, how educated you are, or who your parents are. No matter who likes you and who doesn't, no matter what you have or don't have, no matter what you've achieved or haven't achieved. It is for people who come from every social class, every culture, and all educational levels. It is for those who dropped out of school as well as those who have earned a doctoral degree or two. It is for individuals who are independently wealthy and for those who live from paycheck to paycheck. It is for those who have successful careers and for those who can't even find or keep a job. This book will show you that the type of esteem you have, *other-dependent* or *self-dependent*, determines whether you experience real happiness that lasts or not.

Now, do you remember that right from the start I said this book is to be experienced? Experiencing this book includes reading the Introduction, completing all *Exploration and Discovery* assignments in the order they are given, plus downloading and reading the free bonus articles that are offered throughout for maximum results. Completion of the *Exploration and Discovery* assignments is crucial to a positive outcome. They are designed to initiate change through new and intentional experiences. They will guide you through your own personal self-exploration about how you were taught to be other-dependent instead of self-dependent. They will help you discover who and/or what outside of yourself you depend upon to make you happy. They are designed to clear up the confusion about what you think you need and what you believe you must have to be happy—and why it keeps changing. And they will help you understand why once you have what you think you need to be happy it doesn't make much difference in the way you feel. Ultimately, these assignments are designed to help you discover how to be self-dependent and experience real happiness from the inside out. They are designed to show you how to be Good With Me.

You won't always know exactly what to do with a particular assignment. If that happens, just do something. There is no right or wrong way to complete it. A website has been created to assist you with your Exploration and Discovery. You can go to www.goodwithme.com/resources/exploration to receive guidance.

It is important to make your *Exploration and Discovery* assignments your own personal experience and to complete them as honestly as possible.

Remember, it's all about experience, experience, experience and practice, practice, practice. No shortcuts allowed!

If you skip over any of the *Exploration and Discovery* assignments, you will cheat yourself out of an opportunity to make the life changes that lead to feeling good and being happy for real. Don't do what you have always done in the past—saving your *Exploration and Discovery* assignments for later when you think you will have more time to complete them. You know what that usually means. You won't do them at all. And nothing much will happen for you other than you will have read another book, acquired more left-brain information, and your life will remain the same. You undoubtedly have already experienced plenty of that.

So let's get started! By the way, don't be surprised that you experience plenty of "Aha" moments and insights as you complete the *Exploration and Discovery* assignments. Here is your first opportunity to experience self-exploration and discovery.

### EXPLORATION AND DISCOVERY:

What do you want to gain from this book? That's right. What do you want to get out of it? What is your reason for picking it up in the first place? Write it down or make a list so you don't lose focus of your purpose.

Another important feature of this book is that there is plenty of space in which to complete your *Exploration and Discovery* assignments. Feel free to write in the space provided. Feel free to write wherever you want. Take ownership of it by making it yours. Through self-exploration:

- You will discover what you already think and believe about happiness.
- You will discover what you have been taught about happiness.
- You will discover the difference between self-dependent happiness and other-dependent happiness.
- You will discover that no person, no material possession, or anything else outside of yourself will ever make you happy for real.
- You will discover that you don't have to live up to everyone else's expectations for you in order to be good enough.
- You will discover that you don't have to put your life at risk to feel better.
- You will discover how the Four Attachments affect your life and interfere with real happiness.
- You will discover how your thoughts create the way you feel: happy or unhappy, good or bad, glad or sad.
- You will discover how to be happy whenever you choose.

Through self-exploration you will discover how to:

1. Monitor and change your thoughts to change the way you feel and behave.
2. Manufacture good thoughts about yourself that are not dependent upon anyone or anything outside of you.
3. Have fun without engaging in your addictions and other risky behaviors.

You must master these three skills to achieve the results you desire. So if for any reason you think you can get what you want from this book without engaging in your own *Exploration and Discovery* process, think again. If you have not already completed your first *Exploration and Discovery* assignment, go back and complete it NOW.

Once that is complete you are ready to continue. But before continuing on, here is a brief preview of what is waiting for you in the pages that follow.

**Part One: *Life Inside My Box.*** This section describes how limited life becomes for individuals who are other-dependent. You will learn that there are two esteems: *other-dependent esteem* and *self-dependent esteem*. You will have the opportunity to explore the Four Attachments that result from other-dependent esteem and how they are responsible for a lot of unnecessary worry and stress. You will discover how to recognize your other-dependency and the Four Attachments and the way they are playing out in your own life by paying attention to your thinking. Recognition of your thoughts is the first step to making the shift from unhappiness to real happiness.

**Part Two: *How Did I End Up in My Box?*** This section provides answers to any questions you may have about how you ended up with other-dependent limitations and unhappiness. It defines what it means to be happy or unhappy and explores the price of other-dependent unhappiness and addiction. It makes the distinction between the real problem and symptoms of the real problem. It addresses the need to escape from unhappiness and shows you how to identify the abnormal escape mechanisms you have normalized in your quest for happiness. It explores what you are doing now to feel good and how you have learned to pretend that you are happy just like everyone else.

Part Two provides a foundation for identifying your own poor choices as a result of depending upon someone or something outside of yourself to feel good. It reveals a step-by-step process that leads up to coming out of your box in Part Three.

**Part Three: *Coming Out of My Box.*** This section reveals how to celebrate yourself for who you are! It shows you how to make a shift in the way you think about yourself. You will discover that a single thought makes a difference. When your thoughts about you change, the way you feel about you changes too. You will be given strategies to practice thinking good thoughts about yourself to feel good about you for the long haul. You'll be given techniques to build your own self-dependent esteem by relying upon yourself instead of depending upon others to give you esteem. And you'll be given a formula to measure your success.

**Part Four: *I'm Out of My Box!*** This is the finish line to becoming a self-dependent Good With Me person. It defies conventional conditioning by teaching you healthy selfishness, shows you how to stop resisting inner peace, and outlines a plan for moving forward by letting go of any other-dependent residue that still remains—the ideas you have been taught about who you should be, what you should be, and what you should have in order to be okay. It reiterates that the way you think about yourself is the real secret to happiness and shows you how to be your own cheerleader. It provides you with a strategy to reinvent who you are so that you are out of your box for good!

# PART ONE

# Life Inside My Box

Life is small for those who have no true self-esteem. Life is so limited without self-esteem that it feels small and confining, like living inside of a box. Life inside the box becomes the only thing they know because they have created their own set of rules that keeps them there. These rules allow them to make excuses for their "boxed-in" lives. Most become resigned to the idea that this is as good as it gets and stay with what is familiar even though it is nowhere near what they want. Let's begin an exploration of life inside the box with the two esteems.

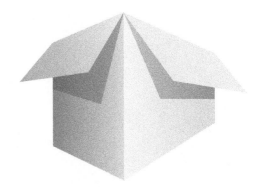

CHAPTER TWO

# The Two Esteems

T he way you feel about yourself is commonly referred to as ***self-esteem***. Let's begin with a simple definition. Esteem as a noun means respect and admiration. Esteem as a verb means to respect and to admire. With that in mind, a simple definition of self-esteem would be self-respect and self-admiration.

In the broadest sense, self-esteem is that which encompasses both self-worth and self-confidence (*Hierarchy of Recovery* by Robert S. Helgoe, PhD). Trzesniewski, Donnellan, and Robins define it as an individual's subjective evaluation of their worth as a person. They further state that, "If a person believes that she is a person of worth and value, then she has high self-esteem, regardless of whether her self-evaluation is validated by others or corroborated by external criteria."

It has been thought that your level of self-esteem determines your overall experience of life. However, what most people don't realize is that there are two kinds of self-esteem and they are not equal.

If self-esteem is self-worth and self-confidence, it's very important to determine the source of this sense of worth. Do you feel good about yourself just because you're you, or do you feel good about yourself because of something outside of you? In other words, is your self-esteem self-dependent or other-dependent? The fact is that what we often call *self*-esteem is usually *other-dependent esteem*. Other-dependent esteem is entirely dependent upon others or events outside of you. This kind of esteem can depend upon how much people like you, getting good grades in school, having a successful career, being a good parent, having the right relationship partner, and much more. In other words, you feel better about yourself only when others feel good about you or when you can take credit for something good that occurs.

True self-esteem, or *self-dependent esteem,* is *not* dependent upon the way others think about you. It isn't dependent upon your accomplishments and material possessions either. You feel good about yourself simply because you are you. It is based on your self's intrinsic value.

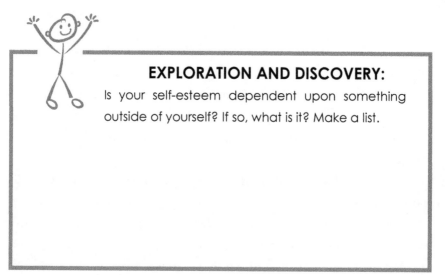

**EXPLORATION AND DISCOVERY:**
Is your self-esteem dependent upon something outside of yourself? If so, what is it? Make a list.

Although most of us have heard of *self*-esteem, few have heard of this distinction between *other*-dependent esteem and *self*-dependent esteem. Including therapists! While most therapists, counselors, teachers, and other professionals have thought they were focused on building *self*-esteem, they have typically been focused on building *other*-dependent esteem without realizing it. We have been promoting the wrong thing without knowing it. That explains why most of society relies on someone or something outside of themselves to have any kind of esteem at all. To continue building *other-*

dependent-esteem is a poor substitute for having *self*-dependent esteem from the inside out, and it results in dependency.

Current research indicates that only 10 to 15 percent of our society has "high self-esteem." The astounding discovery that what we call self-esteem is actually *other-dependent esteem* explains why so few have it. Almost no one knows what real self-esteem is, nor do they know how to have it. As a result, it eludes almost everyone who seeks it. Those who think they have it usually don't. As you know, it's almost impossible to acquire something when you don't know what it is or how to get it.

Anyone without self-dependent esteem knows how crucial it is to be getting plenty of other-dependent esteem. At least you have a reason to feel good about yourself for a little while. But what happens when there is no self-dependent esteem and no other-dependent esteem either? This is the perfect recipe for disaster! This recipe for disaster is being evidenced over and over in our society on a daily basis and will be explained in detail later on.

### EXPLORATION AND DISCOVERY:

What is your idea of self-esteem right now? Write it down so you can compare it with any changes that occur in your idea of self-esteem as you move forward.

Now get ready for a deeper exploration of *self*-dependent esteem and *other*-dependent esteem in the next two chapters.

## CHAPTER THREE

# Self-Dependent Esteem

S elf-dependent esteem comes from the inside out. It means thinking positive thoughts about yourself just because you're *you*. It isn't dependent upon validation from others, successes, or the accumulation of wealth and possessions. This is especially good news for those who don't receive much approval from others, who have nothing, who have not had a success, and are broke most of the time. Many of these individuals give up on ever having anything. Many of them think they are nothing, think they are weird, think no one likes them, and think no one cares anything about them. Some have given up on ever being good enough and have become the lost ones. Some become angry, enraged, violent, and even resort to criminal behavior because they think they don't count. Well, to you the lost ones, you can have self-dependent esteem too!

## EXPLORATION AND DISCOVERY:

Do you consider yourself a person of worth and value just because you exist? Or is your value and worth other-dependent with all sorts of conditions attached to it? If so make a list of the conditions attached to your worth and value. Is your self-confidence dependent upon external criteria? If so make a list of the external criteria.

As we said in the previous chapter, self-esteem is everything. It greatly influences our overall experience of life. And yet for most of us, something this important seems to have little meaning and is a low priority in our lives. Even those who seem to know they have no self-esteem don't give it much thought. It certainly isn't a part of many everyday conversations. We don't usually hear someone say they are having a hard time in their relationship because they have no self-esteem. Most are too busy with other life issues to pay much attention, if any at all, to their self-esteem. Thus very few individuals ever get to realize what life can be like with self-esteem. Some even mistakenly think they have it when they don't. But, unless you truly experience having self-esteem that is self-dependent instead of other-dependent, there is no way to know what it is. Very few realize that life is difficult without self-dependent esteem and is easier, even in the face of major life situations, when it exists because we are better equipped to handle almost any situation.

With self-dependent esteem, we can be free from ever worrying about what others think of us. We can be free from fear and stress, confident that even if we fail, we are still valuable and worthy of love.

If this is correct, then why wouldn't everyone make self-dependent esteem a major life priority? Why wouldn't everyone do everything within their power to make sure they have it? Why wouldn't everyone put self-dependent esteem at the top of their "to do" list? But then again why would they when they don't know what it is or the difference it makes?

## EXPLORATION AND DISCOVERY:

Do you have self-dependent esteem? What makes you think you have it? This assignment is a catch-22 because in a sense you have to have some level of self-dependent esteem to admit you don't have it. If your esteem was fully other dependent, you would have a hard time admitting to anyone—including yourself—that you may not have it all together. With that in mind, be honest with yourself and admit that you don't have self-dependent esteem if that is true for you. See if you can identify the external criteria that are the source of your esteem.

Here is some assistance for this *Exploration and Discovery* assignment. Honest responses to the following questions will help you make an accurate assessment of the type of esteem you have.

- Do you manufacture your own good thoughts about yourself that have nothing to do with what you have, what you know, who you know, what you do, and what you achieve?
- Do you respect yourself from within just because you do?

- Do you admire yourself for no particular reason?
- Do you have good thoughts about yourself that have nothing to do with what others think about you?
- Do you make good choices for you more often than not?
- Do you believe in yourself?
- Would you like to have someone like yourself as a best friend?
- Are you someone who is "what you see is what you get" no matter what?
- Are you happy with you just because you exist?

Take your time with this exploration. Remember there is no need to pretend you have self-dependent esteem if you don't. You don't have to worry about what someone else thinks. Self-honesty is what matters most in moving forward.

Here is a testimonial from Dan, a Focus One participant, that exemplifies happiness just because.

Growing up a redhead I was always the target of elementary taunts, making me feel like I was less of a person because of a simple hair color. It's amazing the lasting effects childhood bullying can have on one's psyche. When it came to high school and college my insecurities came full bore. Always caring what others thought of me and what I was doing. The "cool" kids were drinking, so I was drinking. The "cool" kids were smoking, so I was smoking. I was trying to be normal. After college I chased the money and society's idea of success. I was being the person everybody wanted me to be. And there I was buying into it. Here's the cliché catch though: all the success and money I could have didn't fulfill my lack of security. It didn't get me true happiness. It was the equivalent to putting a Band-Aid on a bullet wound. I was living the idea of

*continued...*

*...continued from previous page*

success on the outside but still tormented with insecurity on the inside.

The stress in our lives is what we create and is often the ending result of us worrying about others and their opinions. This past week I was surrounded by family and friends for a best friend's wedding. Instantly they all could pick up on a new Dan. A stress-free, happy, and smiling Dan was the end result of the progress made through Focus One.

There were numerous times during this past week where I just found myself with an inner peace and happiness for no reason.

It's amazing how simple and powerful being Good With Me can be on your outlook of life. By continuing to be positive at all turns of life, the life I live has been an absolute pleasure. When you are free from the confines of being judged, one can be happy with nothing but the clothes on his back. I have found this to be true, and the resulting lack of inner turmoil produces a certain happiness that only those who truly embrace it will know.

Dan Lopez

Arrogance and bravado are often mistaken for self-dependent esteem, as well as a cavalier disregard for the welfare of others for personal gain. In some circles, self-dependent esteem has even been associated with obnoxious behavior. Self-dependent esteem is none of this. It is not an exaggerated sense of self-importance and superiority, nor is it wishing you were invisible while trying to escape from the eyes of others. Likewise, it is not pretending to be better than everyone else while believing that you aren't. It is not groveling for acceptance and approval from others, nor is it worrying and stressing about what others think of you. None of these behaviors are representative of self-dependent esteem.

**EXPLORATION AND DISCOVERY:**

Do you want to have self-dependent esteem? What do you think will be different when you have it? How will you know when you have it?

When you have self-dependent esteem you still respect and admire yourself even if everything you own is suddenly gone, even if every friend turns on you, even if nothing turns out the way you thought it should, even if you are wrong about everything you thought you were right about, even if others think you look pretty stupid, and even if you are simply having a "bad hair day."

If you are someone who has no self-dependent esteem, chances are pretty good that you depend upon getting some kind of good feelings about yourself wherever you can. That usually means you do whatever you can to get it from someone or something outside of yourself. That means you are other-dependent. You rely upon *other-dependent* esteem for any bit of esteem you can muster up for yourself. If you identify with this, the next chapter will provide you with many insights about yourself and will help clear up any remaining confusion you have about the two esteems.

## CHAPTER FOUR

# Other-Dependent Esteem

A s we said in chapter two, when we say "self-esteem" more often than not we mean "other-dependent esteem." Even professionals confuse other-dependent esteem with self-esteem. Other-dependent esteem is not self-esteem, nor is it self-dependent esteem. With that in mind, let's continue to clear up any confusion about the two esteems.

While self-dependent esteem comes from within you, other-dependent esteem comes from outside of you. Other-dependent esteem originates from the positive thoughts you have about yourself for a particular reason, such as the positive thoughts others have about you. For example, your boss tells you about the great job you are doing. You feel good, right? What if the boss passed by and didn't say anything? How would you feel then? Would you wonder if something was wrong with your work? If so, you might have other-dependent esteem.

Other-dependent esteem is derived from other people's good opinions of you. It includes the compliments and praise you receive from others, your achievement of certain goals and successes, as well as how they are perceived by others. Others may have a good opinion of you because you are popular, well liked by everyone, and connected with all the right people in all the right places. Others may approve of you because you have plenty of money, a chic or enviable lifestyle, or are the winner of a gold medal. You can gain approval from others because of a toned and muscular body, the clothes you wear, your perfect height and weight, looking handsome or beautiful, your clever wit, your intelligence, or just because you are doing a good job, and the list goes on.

We not only interpret the way others respond to us, we interpret the messages we see and hear on television and all other types of advertising media to imply that something is wrong with us if we don't use their products, wear their garments, drink their beer, drive their cars, act in a certain way, or just plain follow their rules. When we have other-dependent esteem, we are extremely vulnerable to the opinions of others. We allow them to affect the choices we make. We allow them to affect our self-worth. We allow them to affect the way we value ourselves.

Of course, other-dependent esteem can temporarily feel like high self-esteem. When things are going great, you may feel great about yourself. Don't be fooled into thinking you have self-dependent esteem when the good feelings you have about yourself originate from someone or something outside of yourself. When other-dependent esteem is the root of your self-esteem, it is transient. This kind of esteem can come and go. That means any semblance of feeling good about you comes and goes right along with it.

Let's be clear on this very important point. It is other-dependent esteem and not self-dependent esteem that varies between high and low. We experience high other-dependent esteem when others approve of who we are or what we do. On the other hand, we experience low other-dependent esteem when no one likes us or what we do. This means that any respect and admiration we have for ourselves is other-dependent as well.

The fact is that anything external to us is not a reliable or accurate judge of our self-worth. The way others think of you is based on how good you look and whether you are the right kind of person—in their eyes! Others may like you because of what and how much you do for them. They may like you because you put their wants and needs above your own, by being a people pleaser and taking good care of everyone around you even if it hurts you. In all these examples, your esteem belongs to "them" or "it" —someone or something outside of yourself. Since it doesn't really belong to you, it is other-dependent and can be taken away at any time, and often is.

Other-dependent esteem can also come from your own eyes. It can occur when you accomplish what you think you are supposed to accomplish, when you think you look good because you are well-groomed, when you have the perfect relationship partner, when you are popular and in great demand by your friends, when you know you are being seen with all the right people in all the right places, or when you have acquired a big enough bank balance. It can come from the way you think about yourself because of your enviable lifestyle or for winning the gold medal. It is still other-dependent esteem because it is how you think about yourself based on the external criteria.

You can garner other-dependent esteem for yourself from your own thoughts about how great you look on the tennis court, how talented you are, how educated you are with all the right degrees from all the right schools, how much you do for others, or because your life turned out the way you thought it should. This kind of other-dependent esteem, even though it is a product of your own thinking and not based upon direct approval from others, is based upon external criteria. You think you look good because of the external criteria and as a result don't even question whether others approve of you. You think you look good, and it is almost a given that others will too.

## EXPLORATION AND DISCOVERY:

What type of esteem do you think you have? Is it self-dependent or other-dependent? Does any esteem you have for yourself depend upon the approval of others? How much of knowing you look good is based upon external criteria?

Let's clear up any remaining confusion right now. Any esteem you have for yourself that comes from anything other than within you "just because you exist" is other-dependent esteem and doesn't last.

Even when you and everything in your life appears to be near perfect, when you have other-dependent esteem the little voice inside you that wonders what do "they" think is always there. The chattering of that little voice is incessant. You know the little voice I'm talking about, the one that doesn't ever rest—at least not for long. The one that keeps on questioning if something you did is good enough—if you are good enough. I'm sure you've noticed what happens to it as soon as any of the things you depended upon to feel good about yourself no longer exist. The voice lets you know what is wrong with you. It can be quite cruel at times. You already know what I'm talking about.

**EXPLORATION AND DISCOVERY:**
How do you feel about yourself when you experience a glitch in the way your life is turning out or when something you depended upon to feel good about yourself no longer exists?

What happens to the way you feel about yourself when your other-dependent esteem is taken away? Does any amount of feeling good about you remain? What happens to the way you feel about yourself when you are no longer held in high regard by others? What happens when you don't look good to others? When the praise, compliments, accomplishments, and possessions are gone, so is your illusion of self-esteem that was fed by your other-dependent esteem. This loss of other-dependent esteem can be devastating. It often results in depression, anger, rage, violence, and even criminal behavior or suicide.

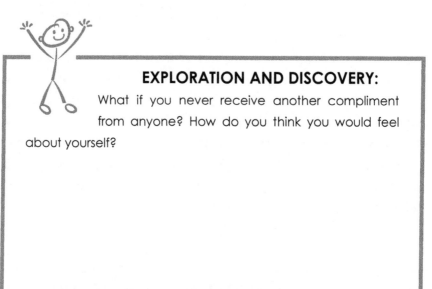

**EXPLORATION AND DISCOVERY:**
What if you never receive another compliment from anyone? How do you think you would feel about yourself?

Once we understand the concept of other-dependent esteem, most of us realize that the only good feelings we have about ourselves are dependent upon others. This dependency upon the approval of others is at the root of the Four Attachments.

## CHAPTER FIVE

# The Four Attachments

*The root of suffering is attachment.*
**—Buddha**

A s we learned in the last chapter, people with other-dependent esteem feel good about themselves only when they have approval from others or think they look good to others This need to be liked by others greatly influences the choices they make. In fact, they become controlled by their need for approval in much the same way an alcoholic becomes controlled by alcohol. Poor choices are often the result.

In particular, people with other-dependent esteem become slaves to the Four Attachments:

- the need for approval from others
- the need to look good
- the need to be right
- the need to control outcomes

All four of these attachments are intertwined and each is dependent upon the other; each one is equally important.

Because individuals with other-dependent esteem need constant approval from others, they continually worry about what others think of them. This constant worry causes an enormous amount of stress. This applies not only to physical traits such as body appearance, wardrobe, hair, skin, weight, and height, but also to intangible traits such as being socially acceptable, socially appropriate, worthy, successful, and accomplished. This intense need to look good to others fosters the need to always be right about everything, which leads to the need to be in control of the way things turn out. All of these needs, or attachments, are fueled by other-dependent esteem.

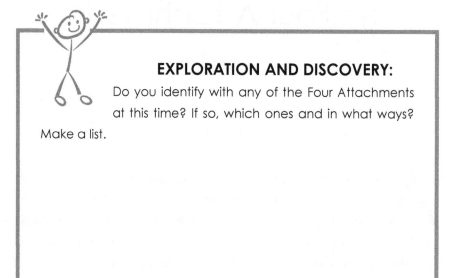

**EXPLORATION AND DISCOVERY:**

Do you identify with any of the Four Attachments at this time? If so, which ones and in what ways? Make a list.

An in-depth explanation of each of the Four Attachments will be presented in the next four chapters.

## CHAPTER SIX

# Attachment #1: The Need for Approval from Others

*Nobody can make you feel inferior without your consent.*
**—Eleanor Roosevelt**

W hat do you think others are thinking about you? Does it matter to you what they are thinking? If so, how much does it matter and why?

**EXPLORATION AND DISCOVERY:**
Before going any further, see if you can identify what you think others think about you. Make some notes to revisit at a later time.

The approval from others does matter to most of society. Why does approval from others matter so much? When we have a poor opinion of ourselves, it is imperative that others have a good opinion of us. We worry about the opinions of others and use them as feedback to determine how we see ourselves. We depend upon the opinions of others to tell us we are good enough—or not.

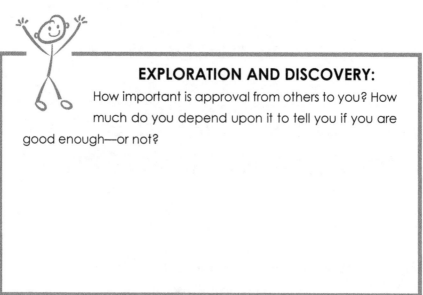

**EXPLORATION AND DISCOVERY:**
How important is approval from others to you? How much do you depend upon it to tell you if you are good enough—or not?

When we don't realize we are good enough just the way we are, we don't trust our own opinions. So we give more value to the opinions of others than to our own. We depend upon others to give us the approval we crave because we are unable to give it to ourselves. In fact, the approval we need has to come from others or we go without. We more often than not allow the opinions of others to sway the decisions we make and don't even ask ourselves why we do it. Most of us don't even realize we're doing it. It's just what we do.

For example, have you ever tried on an article of clothing at a retail store and thought you looked pretty good in it, but you hesitated to buy it because you doubted your own opinion? Did you need someone else's opinion first? Perhaps you did the obvious and asked the sales clerk for an opinion. What made you need an opinion from the sales clerk prior to making the decision to buy? Why wasn't your own opinion good enough? Once the sales clerk, probably a total stranger, validated that you looked great, you made your purchase. You bought an article of clothing based upon the way the sales clerk thought you looked in it.

And what happened next? You got home and your spouse, sibling, or parent didn't like it on you. Uh-oh! Now what? Since you want them to approve of the way you dress, and you value someone else's opinion more than your own, you wondered what you were thinking when you bought this piece of clothing. There is no question that you doubt your own opinion, but you no longer trust the sales clerk's opinion either. After all, she probably works on commission and only said it looked good on you so she could make a sale. So you decided to return it to the store, all the while hoping the same sales clerk wouldn't be there when you did. What would she think of you?

### EXPLORATION AND DISCOVERY:

How important are the opinions of others about you? Do you allow other people's opinions of you to determine the choices you make? Whose opinions do you value more than your own? Have you let them influence the career you pursued, the kind of house you live in, the car you drive, or the people you choose for friends? Do you let the opinions of others affect what you wear or even what you eat? Make a list.

Someone else's opinions of you could affect seemingly unimportant choices too. They might influence your decision to denounce your favorite color, your favorite flower, or your favorite song in favor of someone else's favorite.

If you are thinking that you don't allow the opinions of others to influence your choices, I want you to think about all the times you purchased any kind of advertised product. Add them to your list.

When we allow someone else to tell us what to do, how to look, what to think, etc., we not only give up who we are to gain approval from others, we put our own identity in jeopardy to get it and end up feeling worse about ourselves as a result. And for many the price of worrying about what others think is more than just the loss of identity. By taking these blows to our identity over and over, we go deeper and deeper into the abyss of other-dependent esteem.

The abyss of other-dependent esteem can lead to anxiety, depression, insecurity, envy, fear, more worry that leads to stress, and numerous other misery-making emotions, all of which reinforce the need for even more approval from others.

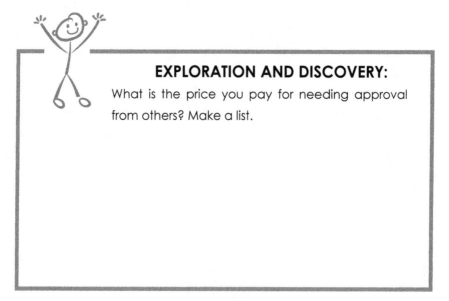

**EXPLORATION AND DISCOVERY:**
What is the price you pay for needing approval from others? Make a list.

Unfortunately, approval from others matters so much to some individuals that they lose their own identity by becoming *people pleasers*. They believe that pleasing others is the only way to get the approval they need, and they will literally do whatever it takes to get it. They will say yes when they really want to say no. And then because they can't say no, they end up resenting the person doing the asking.

An interesting phenomenon occurs when you don't own responsibility for taking care of yourself. You end up resenting the very ones you are trying to please, even though you made the choice to say yes. You may even resent them for asking you for yet another favor. You blame them for the fact that you're doing for them what you don't want to be doing. You make it their fault that you don't have any time for you. You become a victim of your own need for approval from others. What you don't realize is that people have a right to ask for what they want from you and you always have a right to say yes or no.

## EXPLORATION AND DISCOVERY:

How often do you say yes when you really want to say no? Make a list. Do you resent others for asking?

The need for approval that cultivates our worry about others' opinions of us begins early in life. It doesn't take long for us to realize that approval from others has conditions attached to it. As young children we do our best to please our parents and gain their approval. As teenagers we are mostly into pleasing our peers so we can fit in and belong. As young adults we put our best foot forward to please our friends or to hit it off with the right clique. As adults we may do something we don't want to do or even believe in doing just to please a relationship partner or an employer. We might even pursue our parents' aspirations for our life even though it may not be what we want for ourselves at all. But we comply simply because we don't want to disappoint them and lose their approval.

For example, what if your parents wanted you to be a doctor and you chose to go to med school even though you can't stomach the sight of blood? What if you were expected to follow in your father's footsteps in the family business and you had aspirations of your own that didn't include the family business? Now what?

People who worry about the opinions of others become chameleons and life becomes a juggling act. They are always changing, and usually faking, their likes and dislikes to gain the approval of others.

## EXPLORATION AND DISCOVERY:
What were you expected to do or be that you didn't want for yourself? Did you comply? If so, why did you comply? Make some notes to review later on.

A client, Matthew Lawandales, says the following:

In my life, I have many relationships—personal, professional, social—and in each there are people who I allow to diminish my self-esteem/self-worth. What makes it worse is some of those people are

*continued...*

*...continued from previous page*

family members, parents, long-term friends, and even my girlfriend. Whether my allowance of this has been intentional or not, I have to break the pattern of seeing myself through their eyes otherwise I'll continue to have no self-esteem. Instead of giving these people permission to judge me, I need to give myself permission to be responsible for my happiness/ worth. It's tough for me to grasp this because all of my life I've been conditioned to care more about the opinions of myself from other people than from myself. For example, what I think will be the hardest to let go of are the opinions of my parents. It's not atypical to want to make parents proud of you, whether that be with school, sports, etc., but now that I really look into it, it doesn't matter because it's not their life, it's mine. The people who I've let dictate my happiness are only limiting the true potential of my happiness/self-esteem. It doesn't matter what anybody thinks about what I wear, look like, the car I drive, the job I have, the house I live in, or the money I have, except me. All those things that we've been conditioned to think determine who/what we are at the end of the day are meaningless. What matters most is how I see myself and I love Me!

Because we are forever trying to please everyone so everyone will have a good opinion of us, we forget—or worse yet, we never really know—who we are or what it is we want for ourselves. We simply want what we think everyone else thinks we should want. As a result, few people actually know what they want although they can recite a litany of things they know they don't want. Not knowing what you do want makes getting it nearly impossible.

Matthew agrees:

Personally I can relate from a young age. In my family you go to college, no questions asked, or you're considered a failure. I did go to college and was studying pre-law because, again, in my family of doctors and lawyers, you're one or the other. I ended up wasting two years of my life and money taking classes to become a lawyer until I realized that was just what other people wanted. I changed my major to international affairs, which was more business related, then got into IT recruiting. I love my job and am truly happy because I did it for myself, not anybody else.

### EXPLORATION AND DISCOVERY:
Make a list of what you *do* want. Every time you think of something you do want, add it to the list.

The need for approval can lead some to engage in behavior that contradicts their personal values and morals for the validation they need. There is nothing they won't do to get that validation. We often refer to this poor choice of behavior as succumbing to peer pressure, and it drives both teenagers and adults.

It could be the high school student who chooses to skip school and smoke pot with his peers for their validation. Or it could be the individual who embezzles money on the job just to keep up with the Joneses. Both are ignoring their personal values and morals at great risk to themselves so their peer group will have a good opinion of them. They aren't thinking about what anyone will think if they get caught. Or maybe they are and this nagging fear is exhausting, but they are willing to endure this misery because of their more urgent need for immediate validation and approval. The need for the good opinion of others and the validation that results from looking good on the outside in the moment wins.

### EXPLORATION AND DISCOVERY:

How have you contradicted your values and morals just to make sure someone, especially your chosen peer group, has a good opinion of you? What were the results of your choice to do so?

Some people seem to have totally given up on approval from others—claiming they don't care what others think of them. They make it very clear they have no interest in the opinions of others. In reality, this is their roundabout way to elicit a good opinion from others. They assume that others will have a good opinion of them because they don't care what anyone thinks about them.

**EXPLORATION AND DISCOVERY:**
If you have given up and don't care what others think about you, be honest with yourself. Is it because you have esteem for yourself, or is it a roundabout way for you to "wow" others into having a good opinion of you?

On a positive note, asking others for their opinion is not always related to other-dependent esteem. People who enjoy self-dependent esteem are not afraid to ask someone else for an opinion. Since no one person knows everything about everything, the individual who has self-dependent esteem is not fearful of having someone find out they don't know everything. It doesn't even occur to them that someone might have a low opinion of them because they don't know something. They view the opinions of others as helpful in their decision-making process. They don't fear looking stupid. They actually reach out to others for their opinions because they know how valuable the opinions of others can be. And they are able to accept what is valuable to their decision-making process and ignore what isn't.

An example of this positive use of others' opinions is one most of us have probably experienced. Do you remember a time when you were sitting in a classroom and didn't understand what the instructor had just presented? Did you raise your hand immediately to ask what she meant? Or were you among the majority who didn't raise their hand for fear of looking stupid? You might have thought that everyone else probably knew what she meant and you were the only one who didn't. Right? Do you remember the relief you felt when someone finally did ask the question that you and most of the class wanted to ask but didn't?

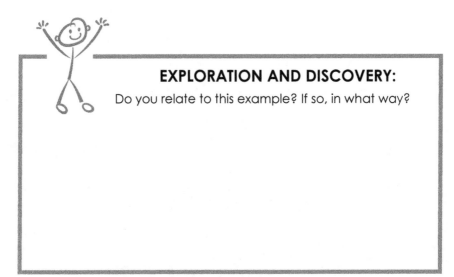

**EXPLORATION AND DISCOVERY:**

Do you relate to this example? If so, in what way?

When we need to have others think well of us because we don't think well of ourselves, we not only need approval from others, we have another powerful need going on simultaneously: the need to look good to others. After all, how can others approve of us when we look bad? This is the second attachment, which we'll cover in the next chapter.

## CHAPTER SEVEN

# Attachment #2: The Need to Look Good

The second attachment, the need to look good, results from the first attachment: the need for approval from others. In general, without self-dependent esteem, one way to make certain that others have good thoughts about us is to look good at all times, in every situation, and to everyone.

Looking good has an entirely different meaning to different individuals. For some it could mean being seen with the lowest of the low and the baddest of the bad, just as easily as it could mean being seen with the rich and famous for others. Looking good, to some, might mean they aren't afraid to hurt someone. For example, it could be the school bully who thinks she looks good when she makes fun of someone who appears to be "different" and is too afraid to stand up for herself. For someone else it might mean being loud and obnoxious. For a few it might mean gunning down innocent individuals to make a name for themselves.

Looking good to you might mean hanging out with those who participate in risky or illegal activities. It could mean taking on a dangerous challenge or participating in a crime just to show how tough you are—and to look good. A former gang member reflects on the need to look good when he says, "Why do we kill each other over a color and three letters?"

It could even mean hanging out with other alcoholics or drug users at the local neighborhood bar or fancy restaurant. Or it could mean that you are the caretaker who sacrifices himself for others or the overachiever who studies, practices, or works 24/7 to look good. How many different ways are there to look good?

### EXPLORATION AND DISCOVERY:

What does looking good mean to you? What have you done in the past to look good? What are you doing right now to look good? Make a list.

For some the need to look good is deeply ingrained because of a family's historic need to look good that has been passed down from one generation to another. In fact, most of us learned early in life that it is important to look good, beginning with our physical appearance. A seemingly innocent comment from a parent who instructs us to stay clean while eating our ice cream cone and scolds us when we get ice cream all over our face and clothes gives us a profound message about the importance of looking good. We quickly learn that looking good is connected to the approval of others. And it doesn't take long for us to associate looking good with more than personal appearance and clean clothes. We learn to attach it to popularity, accomplishment, success, wealth, social status, and a host of other important and unimportant characteristics.

In other words, any positive thoughts we have about ourselves seem to be present only when we think we look good to others. Could that be true? Yes. However, when the good thoughts we have about ourselves are dependent upon someone else, feeling good about ourselves doesn't last long.

Let's examine this concept. Who defines the way we need to look to "look good"? What influences our perception of what it means to look good to ourselves and to others? For one thing, the media usually tells us how we are supposed to look. Television commercials, magazine ads, radio campaigns, and even billboards tell us which trendy labels we should wear, not just on our clothes and shoes, but right down to our underwear. We are not only bombarded by messages about what we should wear, but also what we should own to look good. These standards for the approved good life include everything from the kind of car, house, neighborhood, country club, career, and even brand of breakfast cereal we should desire. Advertisers very cleverly suggest to us that certain brands of perfume make us sexy and desirable, just as drinking the right kind of beer or liquor makes us look cool and attractive to others.

### EXPLORATION AND DISCOVERY:
How much do you allow the media to influence your definition of looking good? Make a list.

Indeed, advertisers send messages that tell us what we should do to look good in a very discriminating society. And we believe them!

Since we don't feel very good about ourselves and are dependent upon someone or something outside of ourselves to make us feel good in the first place, we think these advertisements hold the key to looking good which, in turn, will make us feel good. We place so much stock in their promises, off we go buying one of this and one of that to look good, as promised.

The advertising media has one goal: to create a message that speaks directly to our need to look good, to our need to be like the models who have an army of professionals to style them, light them, and Photoshop them until they are totally fictional characters—and we buy right into their messages. We succumb to the calculated influence of advertising and do exactly what they want us to do. We do whatever it takes to emulate the "beautiful people" to look as good as they do. We believe that once we have those fashionable jeans, are wearing a sensual perfume and our chic underwear, while driving the perfect car and showing up at all the right places, we will definitely look good. Of course, once we do all this it should make us feel good, right? Wrong. Why not? Even with all "the right things" advertised to make us look good, feeling good about ourselves just doesn't last when the feeling is based on temporary external fixes. They are just a Band-Aid. They don't change the root cause of our need to feel better, so feeling good about ourselves doesn't last.

But there's another reason these feelings don't last. What the promoters of every kind of product don't advertise is that as soon as you buy that pair of expensive jeans, that sexy perfume, or that new car, the styles change. This year's fragrance is sexier than last year's. New models of automobiles are unveiled. Then what? Does that mean we have to buy the latest style, sexy fragrance, or newer model to continue looking good to others? You know the answer to that as well as I do. Of course it does. That's what you think you have to do to look good. Your friends and neighbors expect it of you. On the other hand, consider the idea that there is not a pair of jeans, a bottle of perfume, or a new car anywhere in the world that can truly make anyone feel good for very long. The temporary guidelines determined by society (remember, the guidelines are always changing) create a temporary sense of looking good which makes us feel better temporarily. And even if the guidelines stayed the same forever, the sense of feeling better would still be temporary because our self-esteem is dependent upon something outside of ourselves.

Having all the right things to look good won't make us feel good about ourselves for real and it won't make us happy for real either. We might feel good about all our possessions, but that is quite different from feeling good about ourselves. The way we feel about our possessions won't give us self-dependent esteem or feelings of self-worth from the inside out.

Remember: when nothing changes, nothing changes. Just because we change what we wear, drive, or own doesn't mean we've made the changes on the inside that would allow us to feel good on a permanent basis.

When we rely on looking good to feel good about ourselves, we gauge how good we look by comparing ourselves to others. Comparing is so common today that we have coined a new word, *comparanoia,* to illustrate the magnitude of the unhealthy, obsessive comparison of ourselves to others.

Go to www.goodwithme.com/resources for a bonus article and to learn more about the "Comparanoia Slaves."

Comparing ourselves to others is a no-win situation. Individuals who are other-dependent almost never compare themselves to someone they see as less than themselves, unless they do so as a way to make themselves look better. Instead, they almost always compare themselves to someone they think looks better, and sadly they find themselves lacking. In their own opinion they don't measure up and don't look good enough.

My client Richard says:

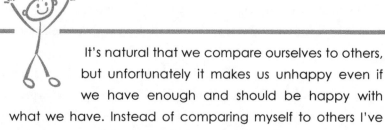

It's natural that we compare ourselves to others, but unfortunately it makes us unhappy even if we have enough and should be happy with what we have. Instead of comparing myself to others I've created the habit of comparing myself to myself. I look back at when I started my journey toward my goals and realize how much I've grown, achieved, and the progress I have made toward my goals. This habit gives me the benefit of

*continued...*

*...continued from previous page*

creating gratitude, positive reception, and consideration toward myself as I observe how far I've arrived at stopping my negative comparisons to people. I feel good about myself without having to think less of other people. I will always know I will never be the fastest, the strongest, the smartest, the biggest or smallest, or any other extreme in life. I know I'm middle of the road and I don't mind being there. I am not jealous of anyone, but there are those who want to make me want to be better. In the end I must be happy being me and happy for another's success at being themselves. I don't focus on how I rank in comparison to others; life is not a competition it's a journey. My journey has nothing to do with how well other people are doing or what they have. It has everything to do with what I want to do and where I want to go. That's all I need to think about.

We learn from an early age that we only look as good as our "stuff." This stuff includes not only what we own but what we do, what we have achieved, who we know, our physical appearance, and the list goes on. We are taught to compare the way we look with those who have more money than we have, a better career than we have, a better education than we have, are more important than we are, and are prettier than we are. And then, because we have no self-dependent esteem, we condemn ourselves for not looking good enough. A June 5, 2011, report on CNN confirmed this phenomenon. The program cited that the more young girls watch TV and celebrities, the more they hate their bodies.

## EXPLORATION AND DISCOVERY:

What about yourself do you compare to others? Do you compare your education to theirs? Do

*continued...*

*...continued from previous page*

you compare your dysfunctional family to their well-adjusted family? Do you compare your nose to hers? Do you compare your thinning hair to his thick hair? Do you compare yourself to the "beautiful people" or the "important people" who appear on the covers of magazines? Make a list for yourself.

For many, looking good is not exclusively influenced by the material items that money can buy or how they look in the clothes they wear. Looking good is often based upon the people with whom they associate. It's about having the right kind of parents or the right kind of kids. It can even be influenced by having the perfect girlfriend or boyfriend, or marrying the exact right person. It can mean being seen in the company of important people in business, government, etc. For many, the only way to look good is by being with people who they think make them look good to others.

It might not make much sense, but some of the most successful people in the world have reached their pinnacle of success because of their need to look good. Yes, they too have other-dependent esteem, and a good enough success is never quite good enough. Neither is the next success good enough nor the one after that. They keep raising the bar, and good enough is never good enough to look good to others.

Many who need to look good live in constant fear that someone will glimpse their inadequacies and point them out to others. They fear that others will find out what they already know about themselves. If that happens, they aren't going to look very good. They fear not being liked by others if they are exposed for who they really are.

**EXPLORATION AND DISCOVERY:**

How much of yourself do you deny or try to hide from others to look good and appear to be right?

Is being right on your list of ways to look good? Let's explore the need to be right in order to look good in the next chapter.

## CHAPTER EIGHT

# Attachment #3: The Need to Be Right

Are you someone who has to be right? Are you someone who has to know it all? Do you argue a point to the *nth* degree in order to be right? Do you alienate even the best of friends to prove your point? Have you ruined a relationship or two because of your need to be right?

The attachment to being right is another manifestation of other-dependent esteem. The attachment to being right, just like the attachment to looking good, is grounded in the negative thoughts you have about yourself. When you have to be right all the time, you give yourself the impossible task of having to know it all. In other words, you have to know everything about everything. WOW! What an unattainable task you've given yourself.

**EXPLORATION AND DISCOVERY:**

Are you a know-it-all? How important is it to be seen as someone who knows what you're talking about or what you're doing? Or to be seen as someone who knows it all?

People who'd never dream of disrespecting themselves or anyone else go to great lengths to be right. The need to be right can be so powerful that it's common to see highly knowledgeable professionals and experts arguing during television news interviews just to make their point. Why isn't it okay to simply disagree? What makes it so important to be right that an individual would lose self-control just to prove their point? While the goal is to look good by being right, sometimes we actually give up looking good in order to be right without realizing it.

**EXPLORATION AND DISCOVERY:**

How important is it for you to be right? How have you behaved just to prove a point?

Do you have a hard time admitting you're wrong even when you know you are? Once you realize you're wrong, do you continue to argue your point? Do you feel embarrassed or humiliated when proven wrong? Do you get angry if someone dares to say you're wrong? Do you become abusive either verbally or physically when told you are wrong? Is your reaction to being wrong an over-the-top, inappropriate response because of your need to look good by being right? Or do you react to being wrong by wishing you could "crawl under the rug and disappear"?

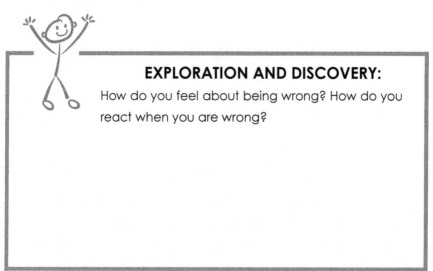

**EXPLORATION AND DISCOVERY:**
How do you feel about being wrong? How do you react when you are wrong?

The need to be right is a serious attachment. An extreme example of the need to be right occurs when nations go to war to be right! How about cultures that annihilate each other because the other culture is wrong? If you would rather suffer any consequence to avoid being wrong, or you'd rather start an altercation to prove you're right, your need to prove your worthiness is a glaring indication that you have no self-dependent esteem.

The fact is that no one knows everything about everything—no one. When your thoughts about yourself are negative, you may be one of those individuals whose thinking falls into one of three possibilities:

1. Everyone else surely does know everything about everything.
2. At the very least, other people know a lot more than I know.
3. Others don't know much of anything at all.

To level the playing field in your own mind, you simply have to know more than the next person. You might even think that others expect you should know "it"—whatever "it" happens to be. How can you impress others and look good if you don't know "it"?

The driving force behind the need to be right is the need to look good because you are worried about what others think of you. How can others have a good opinion of you, how can you look good, and how can you be right unless you are able to control the outcome of things?

That brings us to attachment #4: the need to control the outcome. We will explore its implications in the next chapter.

## CHAPTER NINE

# Attachment #4: The Need to Control the Outcome

The attachment to controlling the outcome is not about *wanting* someone or something to turn out a certain way; it's about *needing* someone or something to turn out a certain way. People who depend upon others for their esteem depend upon everything turning out the way they think it should. Why? Because this is part of what they think they *need* to do to impress others. Controlling the outcome helps satisfy their need to look good and be right as established in attachments #2 and #3 so that others will approve of them as outlined in attachment #1.

**EXPLORATION AND DISCOVERY:**

How important is it to you that everything turns out the way you think it should? Are you someone who worries about the way situations may or may not turn out? Does everything in its entirety need to turn out the way you think it should? Are you overly concerned with outcomes or results?

Individuals who are attached to the way everything turns out generally go to great lengths to make their desired outcomes happen. Control and manipulation are often used to make sure they get their way—to make others do what they think others should do and to have everything happen their way. If necessary, dishonesty can play a part in achieving a desired outcome—their desired outcome.

In your attempt to control an outcome, you might not be obvious or malicious. Some examples of this are crying, withholding, pouting, yelling, or lecturing. Controlling could take the form of emotional, verbal, or behavioral coercion.

**EXPLORATION AND DISCOVERY:**

What do you do to get everything to turn out the way you think it should and get your own way? Be brutally honest with yourself on this one! You may never have
*continued...*

*...continued from previous page*
paid any attention to how unacceptable and inappropriate your behavior is. Realize that your lack of self-dependent esteem and your need for other-dependent esteem can make it nearly impossible for you to identify your unacceptable and inappropriate choice of behaviors. Do the best you can with it. Remember: the more honest you are with yourself, the greater the progress will be toward becoming a Good With Me person.

People who need to have everything turn out the way they think it should and have others do what they think they should are often referred to as "control freaks." These individuals are constantly trying to control people, places, and/or things. They don't realize that it is an impossible task, and they keep on trying—doing whatever it takes to accomplish their desired goal.

### EXPLORATION AND DISCOVERY:

How do you try to control people, places, and/or things? Are you a "control freak"? Do you manipulate? Are you an instigator? Are you the one who needles others with sarcasm to accomplish your goal? Do you goad others into following you? Do you intimidate others into succumbing to your direction?

If you think you are controlling anyone or anything outside of yourself, you are deluded. Even when every once in a while things seem to go your way or someone does exactly what you want them to do, you are not in control of them. You simply have the illusion of being in control.

In actuality, here is what happens. Let's say you really wanted a friend to do something your way. You may have persuaded or coerced him to get your way. When he did it your way, you thought you were in control. Well, not so. He simply made the choice to do it your way. His choice to do it your way gives you the illusion of being in control. He could just as easily have chosen not to do it your way and dealt with the unpleasant consequences. But instead he chose to do it your way perhaps because that is what he wanted to do in the first place, perhaps to avoid any unpleasant consequences, or perhaps for any other reason that works for him. You might think you are in control as a result, but in reality he made a choice that best suited him. So who is in control of whom?

An individual with self-dependent esteem isn't afraid to choose what he wants to do with or without your unpleasant consequences. In other words, he doesn't give in to your "persuasion." You don't always have to agree with him. Therefore, he doesn't have a need to rebel at your attempt to control him. In contrast, the person who is other-dependent rebels at your attempt to control and will often choose to do just the opposite of what you want them to do, even though they might be hurt by their decision. Whenever they rebel, they are not only saying "you can't tell me what I can or cannot do," they are also saying "I'll show you, I'll hurt me."

### EXPLORATION AND DISCOVERY:

What do you do when others don't choose to do what you want them to do? What attempts have you made to control the uncontrollable? Make a list.

People with other-dependent esteem need to control the way things turn out so they will look good and be right, and so others will approve of them—all four attachments are at work all at once.

It should be easy to see how your worry about other people's opinions, along with your need to look good, your need to always be right, and your need to control outcomes can make you sick with worry, which almost always becomes stress. But to understand how worry and stress affect us, we first need to understand how we think. So let's take an in-depth look at the role of thinking in the next two chapters.

## CHAPTER TEN

# Thinking Makes It So

*There is nothing either good or bad, but thinking makes it so.*
—**William Shakespeare**, *Hamlet*, **Act 2, Scene 2**

I t may appear to most of us that life just happens and we have little or no control over what happens or how it happens. But life doesn't just happen. While it's true that circumstances beyond our control do happen, it is not what happens that creates our reality. It is the way we *think* about what happens that creates our own unique reality.

Whatever you think it is, it is. While it has been said that thought is just thought and it is neither good nor bad, if you think something is bad, then it is bad for you. Someone else may think that what you think is bad is good. Who is right? You both are right, because thinking makes it so for each of you—whatever you think it is makes it exactly that for you. Have you ever noticed how differently siblings from the same family perceive the exact same shared experience?

What you think matters because what "you think" about another person, a job, an experience, and even a day, whether accurate or inaccurate, makes it so in your brain, even if your thoughts and perceptions are faulty.

Here's how it works:

- An event happens, or someone says or does something.
- You have a thought about the incident that occurred.
- The way you think about what you heard, saw, or experienced creates your own unique version of what happened.
- The way you think about what happened, not the actual facts of what occurred, determines how you feel about it and then how you react to it.

The way you think about what happened doesn't have to be accurate to be real for you. Once you have the thought, it becomes real for you until you change your thinking about it.

Let's look at a couple of examples of "thinking makes it so." Did you believe in Santa Claus as a child? If you did, do you remember how real he was to you? You defied your friends who told you there was no Santa Claus! They were just plain wrong! In fact, you thought you heard Santa's reindeer on the roof as you were trying to get to sleep on Christmas Eve. Who was right about Santa Claus in this example? You thought you were right and your friend thought he was right. Santa was so real to you that you put cookies out for him and went to bed wondering if Santa would bring you everything on your list. Your friend on the other hand didn't bother with the cookies and went to bed wondering what Mom and Dad had bought for him. You were both right. Each of you created your own reality of Santa Claus as evidenced through your experience, because of your "thinking that made it so."

What about the story of *Chicken Little* who thought the sky was falling because he always looked down at the ground? He created his own unique experience that the sky was falling based upon the thoughts he had while looking down at the ground. Someone else looking up at the sky would see that the sky wasn't falling. Each created a different reality about the sky and both thought they were right. "Thinking made it so," no matter whether the thinking was accurate or inaccurate.

**EXPLORATION AND DISCOVERY:**
Recall a time when you thought a certain way about something and later changed your mind about it. Did you think you were right before you changed your mind? Did you also think you were right after you changed your mind? Which part of your thinking was actually right—before you changed your mind or after? Are you beginning to realize that changing your thinking changed your reality?

For example, you may change your thinking about the clothes you wear when styles change in the fashion world. At first you really like the current fashions and think the new styles are ridiculous. You say to yourself, *I'm not wearing that.* But after a while of seeing the new styles over and over on others, you decide to try them out. You make the switch and love the new way you look. What happened? What changed your experience of the new styles? You changed your thinking about the new fashions, didn't you? Your new way of thinking became your new reality.

How many times have you met someone you thought was unattractive and not your type of person? As a result, you weren't very interested in developing a relationship with him or her. A week later you met up with him or her again and this time you found the person to be very attractive—even fun! What changed? You changed your mind about the person. This is a perfect example of how "thinking, whether factually accurate or inaccurate, makes it so." You thought you were right both times. Whether you were right before you changed your mind or after isn't the point here; the point is that you actually created two different realities for yourself by initially thinking one way and later thinking another way. When you "changed your mind" about him or her, you actually changed your thinking about him or her. Your changed thinking created a different reality. And, by the way, the two different realities regarding the same person are usually based upon the way you were thinking about yourself each time you met. You are more likely to think negatively about someone else when you are thinking negatively about yourself and vice versa.

### EXPLORATION AND DISCOVERY:

Can you remember a time when you thought someone was downright awful? All the while you knew you were "dead right" about him or her until something changed your mind at a later time. What was responsible for your change in attitude toward that person? Which thought was accurate? Do you remember how you might have been thinking about yourself before and after you changed your mind?

This concept not only applies to the way things are or the way they happen, and it not only applies to other people, it applies to you too. In theory, the thoughts you have about yourself are no different from the thoughts you have about anything or anyone else in the sense that they create your reality about who you are. But there is one major difference in the thinking you do about yourself: it is the true source of your esteem and determines whether you are self-dependent or other-dependent.

For example, let's assume it is accurate to say that you are a magnificent musician. However, you don't think so. It doesn't matter that you have superb musical abilities, nor does it matter that others see you as a brilliant musician. You undermine your own abilities with self-doubt and create your own reality that you are a mediocre or poor musician. The converse can be true as well. You may think you are a magnificent musician, but the truth is that you are a mediocre or poor musician. You might just be a legend in your own mind. Either way, it is your thinking that makes it real for you.

## EXPLORATION AND DISCOVERY:

Begin to pay attention to the thoughts you have about yourself. What kind of thoughts are you thinking about you? Make a list. Now challenge your list by determining if your thoughts are accurate or inaccurate. What kind of proof do you have that your thoughts are accurate or inaccurate?

Rene Descartes (1596-1650) said it best: "I think, therefore I am."

Ponder this: What would your reality of yourself and anyone or anything else be if you could not think? Of course, it would be whatever it was, but you wouldn't know what it was. You would have no knowledge of it because nothing can exist in your experience without thought to make it so.

Far too many individuals don't realize it is their very own thinking that creates all the chatter they hear going on inside their heads. Most don't even notice the chatter at all. Most of us weren't taught that we are the ones responsible for the chatter.

Thoughts create your blueprint for the way you experience yourself and everyone and everything else. And they do so with or without your awareness. All thought is powerful whether intentional or unintentional. The thoughts that go unnoticed are just as powerful as the thoughts you think with intention.

## EXPLORATION AND DISCOVERY:

Pay attention to your thinking for a day. Keep a log of your thoughts throughout the day. See if you can notice what kind of thoughts you are having. Can you tell if they are positive or negative? You will have to remind yourself continually to be conscious of your thinking. This will take lots of energy, so don't become discouraged when some of your thoughts get past you unnoticed. You, like almost everyone else, may have spent a lifetime ignoring your thoughts.

Since thinking is crucial to your life experience, and especially crucial to your experience of yourself, let's take a minute to explore how your thinking evolved. Why do you think the way you do? Just like everything else, it all started very early in life.

As children, most of us received a lot of help in the "think-it-over" department. How many times were you told to "sit there and think about what you just did"? This statement usually followed a behavior that was considered bad, inappropriate, unacceptable, or all three. This might seem like a perfectly innocent statement when parents are disciplining young children. Since discipline is defined as instruction or training that corrects, molds, or strengthens the individual, what happens to the child who is instructed to "sit there and think about what you just did" when what they just did was bad? How many times did you think you were bad? Where was the distinction between you and your behavior? Were you being taught to think about the wrong thing? Were you being trained to think about how bad or unacceptable you were instead of how good you were? Do we really want to nurture this kind of thinking? Is it wise? On the other hand, did anyone ever tell you to "sit down and think about how good you are"?

## EXPLORATION AND DISCOVERY:

Sit down and think about how good you are. Repeat this throughout this day and every day for the remainder of your life. Can't think of anything good about you? If not, then make something up and think about it over and over again throughout the day. Don't mistake this for encouraging untrue and delusional thinking. There is something good about every single one of us. Sometimes we just have to find it—and beginning with something made-up may lead you to the truth about the good in you. You could even ask a friend or family member to point out something good about you and think about it throughout the day. Or find a word in the dictionary that describes a good trait or characteristic in you that you had forgotten you had and make it your mantra for the day. Then find a new word to describe a good trait or characteristic about yourself each and every day.

I spend most of my time these days teaching people how to change their realities. Neel Kashkari, former assistant secretary of the treasury, said on CNN, June 5, 2010, that "Reality means more than perception." Assuming this to be accurate, since perception creates reality, what happens to our reality if our perception is flawed? Does that mean our reality is flawed as well?

Yes! Many people live day in and day out with a flawed sense of reality and don't realize it. What they don't realize is that their thinking, no matter how accurate or how flawed, determines their experience of themselves, others, and their world. Thought, and thought alone, determines your very own unique experience of life.

Remember this: Our self-dependent esteem or other-dependent esteem, and therefore our happiness or unhappiness, is created for each of us moment by moment with the thoughts we think. We will explore how thinking creates the way we feel and behave in the next chapter.

## CHAPTER ELEVEN

# So You Think?

*All that we are is the result of what we have thought.*
*The mind is everything. What we think, we become.*
**—Buddha**

We have already established that our reality is determined by our thinking. But did you know that a single thought, good or bad, can set up a continuous loop of thinking, feeling, and behaving?

The loop works this way. It starts with a single thought about someone or something. As a result of the thought, a feeling is formed to correspond with the thought. This feeling then determines your behavior toward that someone or something. Your behavior toward that someone or something then triggers another thought that is influenced by the way you behaved. This thought about your behavior then produces another feeling, and this feeling leads to another behavior. This new behavior influences yet another thought, which creates yet another feeling that leads to yet another behavior, and the loop continues on without end.

This same thinking, feeling, behaving loop can be applied to yourself in the same manner. You have a thought about yourself which produces a feeling about yourself. The way you feel about yourself leads to your choice of behavior. Your choice of behavior influences the next thought you have about yourself, which creates another feeling about yourself, which leads to more behavior, which influences another thought about yourself, which forms another feeling about yourself, which in turn leads to another behavior, and the loop continues on without end.

Here is an example. You think you are a poor conversationalist, especially in a group of people. As a result you feel anxious and nervous whenever you are in a group discussion. Because of your anxiety, you "pre-think" every word you are going to say when it's your turn to speak and you monitor each word as you speak it. You are so preoccupied rehearsing what you are going to say and have paid little or no attention to what has been said that you lose the gist of the conversation. So when it is your turn to speak you say something completely out of context. You then think you failed again and immediately feel stupid. You behave as though you have nothing more to say. You act disinterested in the conversation so you will not be expected to participate. Others in the group may begin to wonder what is wrong with you. You think more bad thoughts about yourself for acting the way you are. You feel even worse about yourself, and your internal critical voice is chattering nonstop, but you pretend that nothing is wrong. And the thinking-feeling-behaving loop continues on without end.

As established in this example, the thinking-feeling-behaving loop fuels the way you see yourself and can work for or against you. It is responsible for self-dependent esteem or other-dependent esteem. Whenever you have a negative thought about yourself, you end up feeling bad about who you are. In turn, when you feel bad about yourself, that negativity is reflected in your behavior, usually by disrespecting yourself and/or others. This can lead to another bad or unkind thought which produces yet another negative feeling about you. Once in the negative loop, escaping can be so difficult it seems almost impossible. You may already be aware of this if you are in it.

The unkind thoughts you have about yourself don't have to be due to something really bad. They could simply be that you don't like the way you look in your new outfit, or you are disappointed in yourself for oversleeping. It could also be that you didn't call your mother when you said you would, or that you ate the last cookie in the cookie jar. All it takes is one negative thought to fuel the negative thinking-feeling-behaving loop.

This loop of bad thoughts leading to bad feelings leading to bad behaviors is a continuous loop of "doom and gloom" unless you do something to change it. The catch is you can't do anything to change it until you become aware that it is happening. Remember, neither feelings nor behaviors occur by accident, even when it may seem as though they do.

- Every feeling has a source: a single thought.
- Every behavior has a source: the feeling that was preceded by a thought.

When you don't know what you are thinking it is impossible to change anything. If you want to change the way you feel you have to become aware of your thoughts. It is a must.

German-born theoretical physicist Albert Einstein (1879-1955) was correct when he said "We cannot solve our problems with the same thinking we used when we created them." Likewise, we can't change our other-dependent esteem with the same thinking we used to create it.

The way you think about yourself is dependent upon the way you esteem yourself, and the way you esteem yourself is dependent upon the way you think about yourself.

## EXPLORATION AND DISCOVERY:

Take ownership of the way you think and feel about yourself. Wake up from your auto-pilot thinking and begin to monitor the way you think about you. What kind of thoughts do you think about yourself? What is the driving force
*continued...*

*...continued from previous page*

behind them? It can be hard at first to identify a thought. If this is the case for you, the way you feel is your clue to the thought you are thinking. Your feelings can help you identify the thoughts that led to them. Identify the way you feel about yourself first. Once you identify the way you feel, ask yourself what you were thinking to create this feeling.

This is how it works. You are going along feeling confident about meeting your new employer when out of the blue you start to feel anxious. Before you feel sick with worry, immediately back up in your mind to see what you have been thinking. A thought always precedes the feeling. You have to identify the thought that has suddenly caused the anxiety and change that thought to something that will make you feel confident again. If it seems impossible to change your thinking, recite a nursery rhyme or the lyrics to a song. This acts as a Band-Aid and will change your thinking long enough to eliminate the thoughts that created the anxiety. You could also recall a prior time when you were feeling confident to change your thoughts that will change your mood.

Now that you have an understanding of how thinking is responsible for feelings, it's time to explore the concept of worry in the following chapter.

## CHAPTER TWELVE

# Sick with Worry

**W**orry might not be what you think it is. It doesn't just happen. Thinking causes worry. Worry starts with a single negative thought. But it soon becomes a habit for those who continue to engage in negative thinking. It is the habit of thinking about all the worst possible outcomes.

The dictionary defines worry as a state or condition causing one to feel troubled or uneasy about some uncertain or threatening matter. What the dictionary fails to tell us is that it is the way worriers think about the uncertain or threatening matter that causes them to feel troubled or uneasy—not the uncertain or threatening matter itself.

Worry happens like this. You start thinking about a future anticipated event or situation. The event or situation can be anything. It could be a blind date, starting a new job, riding a horse for the first time, going out to dinner by yourself, flying in an airplane, deep-sea diving, divorce, home foreclosure, bankruptcy, being fired from a job, or any other life event you can possibly imagine. You begin thinking about some kind of dreadful outcome that in reality might or might not occur. That kind of thinking creates troubled or uneasy feelings that are generally known as "worry."

Unfortunately for all worriers, worry is the most futile emotion anyone can have. Logically thinking, what does it accomplish? Nothing at all. People can make themselves "sick with worry," but it doesn't change anything. Worry doesn't make anyone look good, make anyone right, control the opinions of others, or control the way situations turn out. Worry is not an action. Nothing is resolved by worrying because worrying in and of itself does nothing. Let's use starting a new job as an example of worry being the result of thinking. All the following individuals are starting the same new job, yet each one is thinking differently about it.

Individual #1 is excited about starting this new job because she looks forward to doing something she is passionate about.

Individual #2 is thinking about how this job will be a great steppingstone to move him forward on his career path.

Individual #3 views the job with trepidation because he is afraid his skills are not adequate for the position. He worries that someone might find out.

Individual #4 is dreading the job because she took a position doing something she doesn't want to do, just for a paycheck.

Individual #5 is upset about the starting wage and worried about making ends meet on so little pay.

Individual #6 is extremely grateful for the opportunity to have a job, no matter how much it pays.

Individual #7 is worried about what his coworkers will think of him.

Individual #8 is thinking about ways to prove her abilities to the corporate executives and impress them with her knowledge and experience.

## EXPLORATION AND DISCOVERY:

So who do you think is worried about starting the new job and who isn't? See if you can make the distinction between the worrier and the non-worrier. Remember

continued...

...*continued from previous page*
it is the same job position, same rate of pay, same hours, same everything for every one of them.

Who is thinking themselves into feeling troubled and uneasy about an uncertain or threatening matter? Who is thinking themselves into feeling worried about an anticipated future event or situation?

### EXPLORATION AND DISCOVERY:

Which of the above examples do you identify with? Are you able to see that it is your thinking and not the situation that creates your worry? Write about it.

What is the difference between the worrier and the non-worrier? THOUGHT!

The following example illustrates how worry develops. Imagine that you are stuck in traffic. The traffic is not moving at all or it's moving too slowly for your liking. As a result, you begin to think about all the things that could go wrong today if this traffic doesn't get moving—and soon! You think about what could go wrong if you don't arrive at your destination on time. You think about everything that could go wrong if you are late. You might miss your flight; you might be fired from your job; you might not get the big contract; you might miss the wedding ceremony; you might miss out on dinner; you might be late for the movie; you might be late to pick up your child after school; and the list goes on.

In addition to your initial worry, you soon start wondering what others will think about you because you're late. You worry about looking bad to others if you are late—then you worry that they might be angry with you. You are thinking yourself into a frenzied feeling of worry about the outcome of something that hasn't happened yet and might never happen! Soon your frenzied feeling of worry increases to the point of acting out. Before you realize what is happening, you are name calling, horn blowing, or engaging in any number of inappropriate behaviors. Of course, none of your negative thoughts or behaviors does a thing to fix the situation; therefore your worry is futile.

Someone else in the same traffic situation sits back, relaxes, and waits calmly. This individual knows there is nothing he can do about the traffic situation, so he starts thinking about how to make the day work out in case this slow-moving traffic doesn't get moving soon.

Since the mind is more creative in a relaxed state, this individual is able to think about solutions to the situation. He might check on alternative flights and call ahead to advise of his possible late arrival. He might reschedule an appointment or dinner date. Even though he would rather not be stuck in traffic and would rather not be late, he simply does whatever can be done given the situation. Then he kicks back and continues to enjoy the day knowing that the situation is temporary.

This example shows two people and two different outcomes from the same situation. One is worried, the other is not. Since everyone caught in the slow-moving traffic isn't feeling worried, what is the difference between these two examples? Thinking! Thinking! Thinking! It is not the external condition—specifically the slow traffic—that created worry for one individual and not the other. Therefore slow-moving traffic does not cause worry. If it were truly the cause of worry, then everyone caught up in slow-moving traffic anywhere and at any time would be worried.

One individual thought himself into being worried while the other thought himself into remaining calm. One individual thought ahead to all the possible consequences of being late—all of which were negative—even though none of them had yet occurred and might never occur. This individual was thinking negative thoughts about a future anticipated situation or event. This individual was projecting.

Worry and projecting—you can't have one without the other. Projecting means you think ahead to all the possible consequences of being late—all of which were negative in the first example—even though none of them has yet occurred and might never occur. Haven't most of us been taught to "think ahead"? Haven't most of us been taught to project into the future, to look ahead, to be prepared for anything—usually anything bad?

Of course, it's okay to have a plan in case it's needed, but there is no value in thinking negative thoughts that lead to feeling worried about the outcome of some future anticipated event. Worry won't affect the outcome. It will turn out the way it turns out. This is not to say there is nothing you can do to affect an outcome, but only that whatever planning or preparation you might do, worry is not going to help. Worry paralyzes. Worriers become immobilized and are less likely to take the action that could fix the issue.

Something else happens when you worry. The subconscious mind has no concept of time in the form of the past, present, and future. It only recognizes the present. For that reason it cannot make a distinction between a thought about something that occurred in the past, something that is happening in the present, and something that might happen in the future. That's why it reacts to every thought—whether about the past, present, or future—as if it is happening right now.

You may have noticed that when you think of something terrible that might happen, you not only feel anxious or panicky, uneasy or threatened, but your body responds physically as well. You may get sweaty palms or butterflies in your stomach; you may even become nauseated or experience a sleepless night. The body reacts as though the dreaded anticipated event is happening right now—right this very minute. Your subconscious mind doesn't know it isn't happening right now. If you think it, you feel it and react to it.

An example might be a person who is worried that the judge is going to sentence him to jail. He lives through the horror of being incarcerated every time he thinks about all the terrible things that could happen to him in jail, even if there is no reason for him to ever be sent to jail. Likewise the individual who worries about being fired from his job feels anxious every time he thinks about it, even if he is a good employee who has never been considered for a layoff or firing. By the same token, the wife who worries that her husband might cheat on her lives through his cheating every time she thinks about it, even though it never happens. When the conscious mind thinks it, the subconscious mind reacts as though it is happening right here and right now.

So my question is this: How many times do you want to experience being in jail when it hasn't even happened? How many times do you want to experience being fired without ever being fired? How many times do you want to suffer the emotional pain of your husband's cheating when he has never cheated?

### EXPLORATION AND DISCOVERY:

Recall things you have worried about in the past that never happened. Compare what you worried about to what actually happened. Did you expend a lot of energy being worried for nothing?

Worry begins with a single negative thought. You do have the power to control that single negative thought. It is thought that gives meaning to everything!

**EXPLORATION AND DISCOVERY:**

To eliminate worry, you have to change your thoughts about a situation or person. Instead of thinking about a dreaded outcome, think about the countless ways it could turn out great or at the very least okay. If at first you come up blank with a positive outcome, think about one single thing in life you are grateful for. This is a distraction tactic. Once you have distracted yourself from thinking about a dreaded outcome, the next step is to think about how you would like the circumstance to turn out. Just a single thought is good enough. It might not be easy at first, but you can do it. Remain conscious of your thinking, and whenever you notice yourself having a worrisome thought, think once again about a positive outcome.

For example, you are afraid you're going to be let go from your job. Think about what you do right on your job. Think about a recent positive exchange between you and your boss. Dig deep if you have to and think about a good outcome. You might even tell yourself that your worry is all a figment of your imagination and there is absolutely no reason to worry. If job loss is inevitable because of a company closure, think about how you will find a better job with better pay—right away. You might even begin to think that losing your job is positive. You may have to repeat these steps over and over before they take the place of worry. Of course it goes without saying that the more you do it, the easier it becomes.

Not only is worry futile, it almost always leads to feeling stressed. If you are constantly worried about looking good, pleasing everyone, winning every argument, controlling what others think of you or the way things turn out, you are probably thinking yourself into a state of perpetual stress. So let's explore how stress is overrated in the chapter that follows.

## CHAPTER THIRTEEN

# My Stress Is Killing Me!

Stress! It is highly overrated and misunderstood, especially when there is no such thing as stress in the way we've been conditioned to think of it. You may be surprised to hear me say such a thing, but keep reading.

So what is stress? Prior to the 1920s the word stress meant a physical fight-or-flight response to a life-threatening situation. The psychological definition of stress as "the non-specific response of the body to any demand for change" was introduced in 1936 by scientist Hans Selye (1907-1982), and since that time stress has increasingly become a routine part of life for millions of individuals. The word *stress* has become as common and recognizable as Coke and Xerox. As a society, we experience more stress today than at any other time in history. This increase can be attributed to stress that is primarily psychological rather than physical.

Stress in its historical context meant facing the eye of the tiger, literally fearing for your life. While the contemporary experience of stress varies from person to person, it has grown to include major life situations such as divorce, bankruptcy, foreclosure, job loss, illness, trauma, and death of a loved one as well as everyday routines such as paying the bills, pleasing the boss, keeping a relationship partner happy, picking the kids up from school, fighting traffic, and making dinner. According to the United Nations' International Labor Organization, occupational stress is a global epidemic. We even have stress rating scales to rate the levels of stress caused by life events. And people around the world experience "bad days" due to stress.

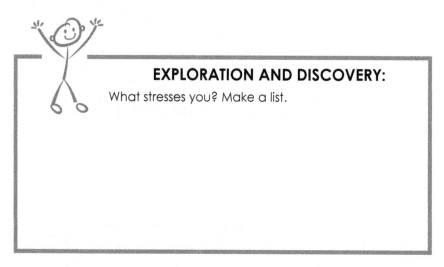

**EXPLORATION AND DISCOVERY:**

What stresses you? Make a list.

*Time* magazine's June 6, 1983, cover referred to stress as "The Epidemic of the Eighties" and America's No. 1 health problem. While it is well documented that stress kills people, it isn't customarily noted as the cause of death on a death certificate. Stress physically weakens the immune and circulatory systems, increases the risk factor for heart attack and stroke, causes damage to cells and muscle tissues, and has a myriad of other debilitating effects on the human body.

Clearly, most people would like to be rid of their stress. This is evidenced by the number of people who participate in stress-management programs. They consult with stress-management experts to learn how to manage their stress more effectively. In case you haven't noticed, there are plenty of stress-management programs and experts available to advise you on managing stress, for a small or not-so-small fee.

**EXPLORATION AND DISCOVERY:**
What are you doing or what have you done to manage your stress or to rid yourself of stress?

More and more people are turning to alcohol and drugs to alleviate their stress. Even Dr. Oz, the internationally renowned cardiothoracic surgeon, author, and television personality of the *Dr. Oz Show*, reported that "the value of alcohol is to get rid of stress..." during a Piers Morgan interview on CNN, May 18, 2012. Yet how many people die from alcoholism as a result of their attempts to manage their stress with it, if only for a little while? Why would anyone want to manage something that might kill them (stress) with something else that could kill them (alcohol), rather than not have the root problem at all?

Clearly people who are other-dependent are stressed to the max. Their worry about others' opinions of them, their need to look good, their need to be right, and their need to control the way things turn out are the root of their stress. This type of stress affects people of all ages, genders, and lifestyles.

I would go one step further and say that other-dependency is *the* cause of stress in our society. So how do we become stress-free? Is this even possible? There are a few among us who do appear to be stress-free. They don't let anything bother them—nothing "ruffles their feathers." You may know someone like that and wonder how they do it. Perhaps the difference between you and them is that they aren't worried about looking good or being right. They don't worry about what others think about them, and they don't need to control the outcome of things. Yep, you guessed it: they have self-dependent esteem.

Other-dependent individuals stress over just about everything. But remember what we said about how thoughts create our reality. Could it be that stress is just a figment of the imagination?

Stress is highly subjective. We don't all think the same way about the same thing. What might be terrifying for one person is not scary at all for another and may be just a little bit frightening for someone else. So since everyone experiences stress differently, what is it that makes people experience certain events as stressful? It all depends on whether we think of an event or an experience as a threat—when our thinking turns it into an "imaginary tiger" in our mind. We experience psychological stress whenever we think about these imaginary tigers.

For example, you may think yourself into being stressed to the max when you believe you don't look good to others or you aren't right about something. You may face imaginary tigers every single time you worry about what others think about you or when things don't go the way you want them to or the way you think they should.

Stress is just a feeling created by the way you *think about* people who don't like you, a relationship breakup, a deadline, an overdrawn bank account, a poor credit rating, a flat tire, a category-five hurricane, stage-four colon cancer, or even being shot at and bombed during war. The fact is people who don't like you are just people who don't like you, a relationship breakup is just a relationship breakup, a deadline is just a deadline, an overdrawn bank account is just an overdrawn bank account, a poor credit rating is just a poor credit rating, a flat tire is just a flat tire, a category-five hurricane is just a category-five hurricane, stage-four colon cancer is just stage-four colon cancer, and being shot at and bombed during war is simply that.

Some people actually enjoy the "fight or flight" adrenaline rush of war and violence or flying into the eye of a hurricane, just as others love the adrenaline rush from riding on a roller coaster. It doesn't stress them out— it excites them. Some people refuse to be defeated by a terminal disease diagnosis. They get very focused on being healthy and doing whatever it takes to effect a cure. They know they can't afford to have a single negative or stressful thought when overcoming a terminal disease diagnosis.

Of course, many soldiers are not excited by war and do not enjoy the rush of adrenaline when encountering violence, but they still must routinely face these terrifying "fight or flight" situations. Even they must learn to control and redirect their thinking to leave the battlefield and violence behind them.

Aside from the physiological fight-or-flight response to a perceived harmful event, attack, or threat to survival, the mechanism that makes us stress over any circumstance is the way we think about it and its subsequent consequences. This is not to make light of any set of circumstances. And yet they simply are what they are, even when we'd rather not have them in our lives. The idea that these situations are not stressful in and of themselves is often very difficult to grasp at first. It contradicts everything we have been taught about stress. Virtually all stress, whether we understand it or not, is caused by the way we think about the impending consequences of these circumstances more than the circumstances themselves.

I don't mean to suggest that we wouldn't experience stress if diagnosed with stage-four colon cancer, or if we encountered a tiger coming straight at us on the walkway. Nor does it mean that a soldier being shot at or bombed in a war zone wouldn't experience stress. Even though the bullets and bombs are not sources of stress, the consequences of them are: death to oneself and to one's friends. Most of us would find it difficult to remain calm in any of these situations. Not to say that it can't be done, but that it is more unlikely to happen. In these situations the body's autonomic nervous system kicks in to protect us by telling us to fight the tiger or flee as fast as we can. It's a powerful built-in protective system and it's within us for a reason. Its job is to keep us alive.

Our physical body is designed to handle this kind of short-term acute stress every now and then without too much damage to our physical health. Thus the fight-or-flight response is a good thing. To the contrary, it's the chronic day in and day out, week in and week out, month in and month out, year in and year out stress that kills!

## EXPLORATION AND DISCOVERY:

Think once again about the things that cause you stress. For example, responsibilities, paying the bills, continued...

*...continued from previous page*

the bank balance, the job, the boss, a relationship breakup, physical health, a medical diagnosis, deadlines, a fast-paced lifestyle, or even the trauma of war. A common cause of stress for many women is juggling a job/career, her husband and kids, and her home. Similarly, many who are the head of a family are stressed over being good providers. What are the causes of your stress as you see them now? Write them down.

It can be hard to realize that your stress is the result of your own thinking. The whole idea that you feel stressed out because you are thinking stressful thoughts might even sound ridiculous.

## EXPLORATION AND DISCOVERY:

Allow yourself to be open to the idea that feeling stressed-out means you are thinking stressful thoughts, and that stress is nothing more or nothing less than that. Pay specific attention to the thoughts you are having each and every time you feel stressed. See if you can identify the thought you had that preceded the feeling of stress. The more you pay attention to what you are thinking, the easier it will be to see that the way you think is responsible for your stress. After all, if there actually was an inherently stressful situation or person, everyone who encounters it would have to be stressed by it. Put it to the test for yourself with the following example.

Your boss stresses you out. It might even appear to you that everyone is stressed out by him. As a result, you believe your boss is the source of everyone's stress. If your boss is truly the source of everyone's stress, then everyone who comes in contact with him would have to be stressed out. However, there is probably someone out there for whom he does not cause stress. It might be his best friend, his mother, or his sweetheart. If he were truly the source of everyone's stress, all those people would have to be stressed out by him too.

Since not everyone who encounters the boss is stressed out, he can't be the cause of your stress. So what causes your stress when you encounter him? It has to be something else—and it is. The way you think about him makes you stressed out and nothing else.

### EXPLORATION AND DISCOVERY:

Notice your thoughts and see if you can change the way you are thinking about whatever it is that is stressing you out. This might not be easy at first, and changing the way you think about some situations will be easier than others. As an example, you may be stressing over getting to work on time, so you might change your thinking to *Relax. It is what it is. Everything is going to be okay. Being stressed won't get me there any sooner.* This is not to make you believe it is okay to be late but to realize that being stressed will not change the outcome. When you succeed at changing your thoughts, the feeling of stress will begin to disappear.

For many, being stressed out is a perfect way to get approval from others. When their stress is worse than everyone else's stress, it provides a way for them to out-do their friends or coworkers. They can one-up everyone else with their stressful life and perhaps even gain a little extra respect. Furthermore, having so much stress to deal with can be a great way to fit in and belong with other stressed-out friends or coworkers.

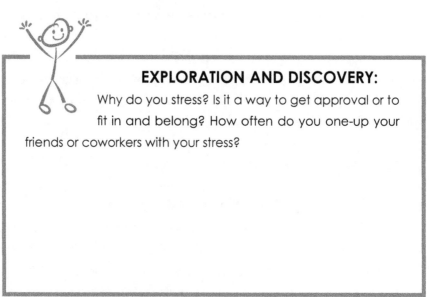

### EXPLORATION AND DISCOVERY:

Why do you stress? Is it a way to get approval or to fit in and belong? How often do you one-up your friends or coworkers with your stress?

Unfortunately, there can be a downside to remaining calm and relaxed. Our society has been conditioned to think that worry and stress equal concern and caring. They equate the depth of your stress to the depth of your caring about someone's poor health, about someone's misfortune, about wanting to succeed on the job, or about anything else for which stress represents the depth of your concern. Society expects you to be stressed to show how much you care.

A lack of stress is sometimes interpreted to mean you don't care. People may think there is something wrong with you unless you are worried and stressed. People may think you are cold and indifferent to the concerns of others when you are not worried and stressed out.

You don't have to be stressed to care; you only think you do because of societal conditioning. You can care deeply about what happens to others while being calm and relaxed. You can feel sympathy for another's misfortune and greatly concerned about someone's safety without being worried and stressed out. Worry and stress have nothing to do with caring. They have to do with negative thinking. In this context, to be sure, stress is overrated!

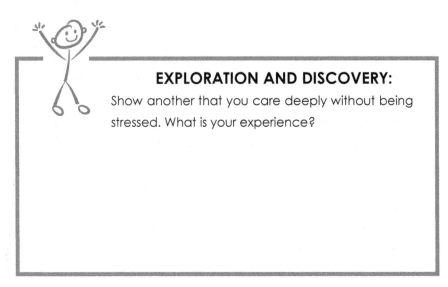

**EXPLORATION AND DISCOVERY:**
Show another that you care deeply without being stressed. What is your experience?

Bad days, like stress, are a result of your thinking. What is real is that you have a day. It is just a day and is neither good nor bad. It is your thinking that makes it good or bad. The same logic applies. If it was a fact that the day was truly bad, it would have to be a bad day for everyone on the planet. Everyone would be having a bad day at the same time, and there would be no way to avoid it. Since not everyone is having a bad day at the same time, it must follow that the day is not bad. So it must be something else that is making you have a bad day. Well, it is something else. It is your thinking that makes it bad.

A bad day starts with a single negative stress-producing thought and spirals downhill from there. This same concept applies to having a good day. A good day starts with a single positive thought and spirals upward from there. You have a choice. What kind of day would you rather think yourself into having?

**EXPLORATION AND DISCOVERY:**

Pay attention to the thoughts you are having about the day. Are they good or bad? Are they stress-producing? If they are good, create more of them. If they are bad, think about one thing that is good about your day. Perhaps it is as simple as waking up this morning. Maybe it is that you have air to breathe or water to drink. You get the idea. Dig deep if necessary to find something good. Even though it might not be easy at first, think about your good instead of your bad. When you notice yourself thinking about what's bad, consciously shift your thinking to what's good. Do this as many times as need be until you are having more thoughts about your good than about your bad. It will become easier with each time you make the shift from bad to good.

Even though a thought is just a thought, neither good nor bad, by the time you feel stressed, it is too late. Let's move on to the next chapter to better understand how important it is to avoid feeling stressed altogether.

## CHAPTER FOURTEEN

# Don't Manage the Damage

D on't manage the damage that is related to stress. The only form of stress management that will make a difference in the way you feel is managing to be free of stress. According to a report from the Chartered Institute of Personnel and Development, stress as a cause of death overshadows stroke, heart attack, cancer, and back problems. According to Beck Barrow, www.dailymail.co.uk, "Experts said the psychological condition [stress] had become so widespread that it was the '21st century equivalent of the Black Death.'" Likewise, Ezine Articles (ezinearticles.com) expert Elisabeth Kuhn writes, "Maybe this sounds a little overdramatic but unfortunately the reality is that excessive, untreated stress can actually kill you." Since we established in chapter thirteen that stress kills, what part of your stress would you really want to manage anyway?

Once we feel stressed out, the damage has been done. The body is already responding to the feeling of stress, and a whole host of negative physical and psychological symptoms have begun. Instead of spending years taking workshops and listening to lectures on how to manage your stress, why not learn how to avoid feeling stressed altogether by managing your thoughts?

The million-dollar question is how do you learn to manage your thinking to avoid creating stressful feelings?

One way to manage your thinking is to use something similar to one of Cesar Millan's (star of the television series *Dog Whisperer with Cesar Millan*, from 2004-2012) dog-training techniques. Millan emphasizes that "you must gain control of the situation and dog behavior before it escalates." Similarly, you have to gain control of your thinking by catching your first negative thought in the act before it escalates into a stressed-out situation. A single negative thought is just a single negative thought until it escalates to more negative thoughts which can very quickly become stress. To gain control you must notice the very first thought of worry, fear, anxiety, pressure, or an impending threat. That is when the first hint of stress begins. To repeat, you have to notice the first hint of a single negative thought—then immediately distract yourself by thinking a single positive thought before that single negative thought escalates to a multitude of negative thoughts that intensify to an unmanageable level of stress. Since feeling stressed out begins with a single negative thought, the sooner you recognize your first negative thought, the easier it will be to change it to a positive thought and avoid feeling stressed.

For example, let's say it's a workday, your alarm failed to go off, and you overslept. You have to catch the first single negative thought, which might be very subtle and may go something like this: *Oh, no—I overslept.* You have to gain control by immediately distracting yourself with a positive thought before this one negative thought takes on a life of its own. Otherwise it can quickly progress to catastrophic thinking. *Did I forget to set my alarm? Oh, no! How could I be so stupid? I will be late! I'm going to lose my job! I won't have enough money to pay the rent! I'll get evicted! I'll end up living under the bridge!* You know where this kind of thinking ends up.

Instead, immediately change your thinking to something like this: *It is what it is. It'll all work out. Everything is going to be all right. It's all good. I must have needed a little extra sleep this morning.* It is important that you don't wait until you are already stressed out to do this. Do it before it escalates into a full-blown stress attack. It is much more difficult to talk/think yourself off the ledge once you are stressed out than it is to distract yourself before you begin thinking a boatload of stressful thoughts. You might want to talk to yourself out loud to change your focus and your thought patterns. When you change your thoughts you will change the way you feel. You will not be stressed out because you are no longer thinking stress-producing thoughts. You will begin to feel calm when you think calm thoughts. Once calm, you can respond to any situation in a positive, relaxed manner. Remember, we are far more creative when we are in a relaxed state of mind.

## EXPLORATION AND DISCOVERY:

Practice changing negative stress-producing thoughts into positive, calming thoughts. Pick a situation in which you would normally become stressed. Identify the type of thoughts you would normally have in that situation. Can you identify the stress-producing thoughts? Once you have identified the stress-producing thoughts, change them to positive, calming thoughts. Create your own personal positive, calming words for this situation and then repeat them over and over again. This is likely to feel strange, even uncomfortable at first, because you are used to feeling stressed out. You might not even believe it is possible to change your stress-producing thoughts to positive, calming thoughts. If and when this happens, just notice that you are uncomfortable and keep on thinking positive, calming thoughts about the situation. Speak the words out loud. Continue this process until you are able to get past your discomfort and your own negative stress-producing thoughts.

How stressed are happy people? Do unhappy people have more stress? Let's take a look at the two happys in the next chapter to learn how thinking happy thoughts is a good antidote for stress.

# PART TWO

# How Did I End Up in My Box?

The answer is both simple and complex. Flawed thinking about who you were during childhood can actually become your truth about who you are. Once you accept your flawed thinking as the truth about yourself, you end up in a box. Simply put, you ended up in your box because of the negative way you saw yourself while growing up. It began with your first negative thought about yourself. Once in your box, unhappiness, addiction, and the need to escape your box prevail. Let's explore what happens in life once you are in your box.

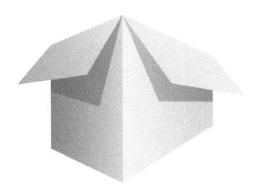

## CHAPTER FIFTEEN

# The Two Happys

Yes, there are two happys. There is real happiness and there is unhappiness. Real happiness is self-dependent while unhappiness is other-dependent. We will discuss both in this chapter.

We've already established that everyone wants to be happy, but who among us even knows what happiness is? How can anyone experience real happiness when most don't know what it is or how to have it? How can anyone experience real happiness when it appears to be a moving target? Just about the time we think we're happy, the requirements for our happiness change and we move onto the next thing we think will make us happy. What we thought would make us happy yesterday doesn't make us happy today.

Most of us define happiness as having the right material possessions, the right friends, the right parents, the right kids, the right education, the right job, the right accomplishments, and all the rest of the next right "you-fill-in-the-blank" stuff. Most of us have been indoctrinated by parents, teachers, social media, the advertising media, and even song lyrics that someone or something out there will make us happy. As a result, we've become focused on acquiring the right things, finding the right person, and doing the right things that are supposed to make us happy.

To this, my client Richard says, "I am not my stuff, not my jeans, not my television, my car, my bank account or my vocation. I think of all of this stuff, and none of it is who I am."

### EXPLORATION AND DISCOVERY:

What were you taught about what it takes to be happy in life? Write it down. Were you told you have to have the right friends (including which ones were right and which ones weren't)? Did you have to find the right relationship partner? How important was it to fit in and belong with the right group of people? Was it expected that you would be popular within your peer group? What about getting good grades in school, the right education, the right degree from the right college or university, graduating with honors, and finally choosing the right career? What about being good in athletics, band, cheerleading? What about wearing the right clothes, especially the right designer labels? What about driving the right automobile, or residing in the perfect house in the best neighborhood? Make a list of what you have considered to be the "right stuff" to make you happy. And don't be surprised if it's a long list.

Of course this list of all the right things is constantly changing. At first we need one of these; then we need one of those, and before long we need more and more of the "right" things to keep us happy. We conclude that more of everything must be what it takes. Before we know it, we have become dependent upon what we think we need to keep us happy, whether it makes us happy or not. We are other-dependent. Does this recipe for happiness really work? Let's take a look.

Let's say you think you need a brand-new car to be happy. You acquire it and are feeling pretty good about having the car. But it doesn't take long until the newness wears off. Ever notice how quickly that new car smell goes away?

Now you start to think about taking an exciting road trip in your new car to feel better. Perhaps you think about buying a motor home for an even better road trip. Or maybe you should stay at better hotels or eat at better restaurants. Have you brought the right clothes for your trip? This process can go on and on.

Is the new car really making you happy? If you have been indoctrinated that brand-new cars make people happy, then your response might be "Yes, it is!" You may even think there is something wrong with you if your new car doesn't make you happy. You might even have to pretend that it is making you happy. So is there anything real about your happiness?

You might begin to think that if this brand-new car doesn't make you happy, perhaps nothing is ever going to make you happy. You even wonder what's wrong with you. Does this recipe for happiness really work? Do brand-new cars or anything else you can substitute for a new car—even another person—make anyone happy? Or do all of those things simply create a temporary illusion of happiness? How would you know?

**EXPLORATION AND DISCOVERY:**
What is your definition of happiness? Remember, it can be whatever it is for you right now. Write it down and save it for later.

Mr. Webster defines happiness as "a state of well-being and contentment; a pleasurable and satisfying experience."

**EXPLORATION AND DISCOVERY:**
What does it take for you to experience "a state of well-being and contentment; a pleasurable and satisfying experience?" Do you even know? Make your list and save it for later.

Do you think happiness is having plenty of possessions even though the rest of your life is in shambles? Have you ever considered that acquiring, being attached to, and worrying about keeping all those possessions could actually be a source of unhappiness? When is enough enough? Is it ever enough? No it isn't—not for the person who is looking for happiness in someone or something outside of themselves.

Happy people are not worried about what others think about them; they don't need approval from others, they don't need to look good, be right, or control the way things turn out. Happy people feel happy because they think happy thoughts. Happy people are happy because they are happy with themselves "just because." They like themselves. They like others. They are not looking for someone or something outside of themselves to validate them. They are not looking for someone or something outside of themselves to make them happy.

**EXPLORATION AND DISCOVERY:**
Are you thinking yourself into being happy? Are you someone who is happy "just because"? Or are you someone who has decided that being happy is just too hard?

If you aren't happy "just because," the chances are pretty great that you are unhappy and might not even know it. Some people don't realize how unhappy they really are. How can that be? For many, unhappiness has become normal. Some think this is as good as it gets while others don't expect to ever be happy. Many unhappy people keep themselves artificially buoyed up with material possessions, successes, wealth, social status, exciting relationships, extramarital affairs, partying, drinking, drugging, and so on. They don't always acknowledge how unhappy they are because they are too busy trying to look happy. They think they need to look happy to look good to others.

Unhappy people are good people who aren't happy with themselves. Unlike happy people, unhappy people are always looking for ways to feel good or at least a little bit better. Deep down inside, they don't like themselves, even though most will never admit it. Because they don't really like themselves, it isn't unusual that they don't like others either—even though they may pretend they do. When people are critical of themselves, they are critical of others. Because they harshly judge themselves, they judge others harshly as well. They engage in behaviors and activities that perpetuate their unhappiness even when their goal is to be happy.

Take a look at the list that follows. Make a check beside each one with which you identify. Unhappy people who do not feel good about themselves:

- ☐ do whatever it takes to look good to others
- ☐ tell little white lies to look good to others
- ☐ live to please others
- ☐ take better care of others than of themselves
- ☐ argue a point to the *nth* degree
- ☐ alienate friends just to be right
- ☐ make themselves sick with worry
- ☐ worry about what others think of them
- ☐ manipulate others to control the way things turn out
- ☐ bully others to get their way
- ☐ are hurtful to others
- ☐ take frustrations out on their spouse, children, or friends
- ☐ have little to no compassion for others
- ☐ become self-centered
- ☐ need a lot of validation from others
- ☐ gossip about others
- ☐ complain a lot
- ☐ need a lot of the right possessions
- ☐ remain employed in a job or career they hate just for the money or social approval
- ☐ cheat to get a promotion or pay raise
- ☐ have excessive spending habits
- ☐ keep credit card debt a secret
- ☐ hide compulsive eating habits
- ☐ remain in abusive relationships
- ☐ engage in self-mutilation
- ☐ participate in unprotected sex with multiple partners
- ☐ turn to pornography for sexual excitement
- ☐ drink and drive
- ☐ use illegal drugs
- ☐ steal for drug money

- [ ] doctor shop by making appointments with numerous doctors to obtain large quantities of medications
- [ ] write fraudulent prescriptions for drugs
- [ ] take part in a variety of risky behaviors (you fill in the blank)

For some, unhappiness is so severe it leads to behaviors that cause divorce, loss of friends, bankruptcy, poor health, loss of reputation, violence, arrests, imprisonment, or death. However, not everyone who is unhappy is so unhappy that they experience such severe and outrageous consequences. They are individuals who seem to go through life with a kind of unhappiness that is "just under the radar." Their unhappiness is not extreme enough for them to do anything about it. Their unhappiness seems minor in comparison to that of others. They often struggle to get through a day and are glad when the day is over. But it doesn't seem bad enough for them to want to make any effort to change. So they don't.

Then there is another group of people who have totally given up on ever being happy. They have decided that life is just too hard, and they do what it takes to suffer through. But of course they will let you know how terrible their suffering is. They feel helpless to do anything about it. Most have even given up on caring about changing, and many resort to drugs and alcohol to numb the pain.

Fortunately, not everyone has given up on being happy, nor does everyone engage in risky behaviors to their complete demise. Neither do they experience such extreme negative outcomes as losing everything. You don't have to get divorced, go bankrupt, or land in jail to have your life disrupted. The negative impact of unhappiness for you could be subtle—so subtle, in fact, that you might not even recognize it.

The following list identifies many subtle negative effects that can be a direct result of your unhappiness. Many of them might appear to be normal everyday events. Which of them do you identify with? Do you:

- [ ] have difficulty getting out of bed in the morning?
- [ ] dread the day ahead?
- [ ] feel relief when the day is over?

- ☐ feel depressed and/or anxious on Sunday night because you dread going to a job you dislike on Monday morning?
- ☐ feel like you're not quite as good as someone else? (you know who that is)
- ☐ pretend to be someone you're not?
- ☐ compare yourself to others?
- ☐ feel like "they" have all the good looks, popularity, fun, success, or even luck?
- ☐ want to trade places with someone who has "more of something" than you do?
- ☐ choose the wrong relationship partner over and over?
- ☐ have a series of failed relationships?
- ☐ want out of the relationship you're in, but stay in it anyway?
- ☐ play too many video games?
- ☐ live your own life vicariously as a Facebook junkie?
- ☐ feel lonely?
- ☐ feel bored?
- ☐ feel weird?
- ☐ feel depressed?
- ☐ feel angry?
- ☐ feel anxious or stressed much of the time?
- ☐ have difficulty relaxing after a stressful day?
- ☐ allow what someone else thinks to spoil things for you?
- ☐ make yourself sick with worry?
- ☐ have emotional pain you want to be rid of?
- ☐ feel like your life didn't turn out the way it was supposed to by now?
- ☐ wait for the "other shoe" to drop whenever something good happens?
- ☐ deal with crisis after crisis?

**EXPLORATION AND DISCOVERY:**
Which of the above do you identify with? Make a list and note how each one of the negative effects usually leads to more unhappiness.

Unhappiness can be costly to your emotional, mental, physical, and spiritual well-being. Let's look at the many ways unhappiness is the price of your other-dependent needs in the next chapter.

## CHAPTER SIXTEEN

# Unhappiness: The Price of Other-Dependent Needs

Happiness that comes from self-dependent esteem is priceless! Unhappiness is the price of other-dependent needs. Other-dependent needs lead to poor choices, plenty of consequences, and ultimately unhappiness. The price of other-dependent needs is costly.

While some poor choices result in "losing it all" as a result of over-the-top destructive behavior, seemingly innocent attempts to fulfill one's other-dependent needs are actually more prevalent. Both come with a price even though some poor choices seem to have no consequence at all. Society may actually view some of these poor choices as admirable. Working way too many hours is a good example of satisfying an other-dependent need even though working hard is seen by many as a good choice. How can working hard possibly be the result of an other-dependent need, especially since work is so highly valued in our society?

When the motivation is the need for approval from others, working 24/7 might be considered a small price to pay. Becoming the classic "workaholic" is viewed by many as an admirable choice of behavior because it shows a good work ethic. This workaholic is outwardly a good provider, is not doing anything wrong, and is often perceived as a "pillar of the community." He even receives kudos for working so hard. Working 24/7 satisfies his other-dependent needs because he looks good to others and receives plenty of approval to boot. After all, he is working and not irresponsibly drinking beer at the local pub or cheating on his spouse waiting at home.

One could argue that this workaholic doesn't even feel good. How could working twelve-hour days, seven days a week feel good? It satisfies the other-dependent need to look good to others even when work is used as a reasonable excuse to be absent from unpleasant family obligations, outings, and even vacations. The motivation for this type of workaholic is not only avoidance but approval from others while doing so.

What about the individual who works 24/7 just to "keep up with the Joneses"? Looking good to others is the other-dependent need of this workaholic. He works hard to make enough money to buy all the "bells and whistles." For this workaholic, the "bells and whistles" make him look good to his family, friends, and neighbors. It doesn't matter that he has no time to enjoy them. It's all about looking good to others. The motivation for this type of workaholic is looking good so that others will have a good opinion of him.

Another workaholic loves her family and says she wants to spend more time with them. However, her other-dependent need to be recognized as the best and hardest worker is more important than the family she wants to spend more time with. She works better and harder than everyone else for the praise and recognition she receives at work. Of course, she likes getting a promotion and a raise too, but above all else she relishes the opportunity to look good, not only to her supervisor, but to her peers. The motivation for this workaholic is looking good to others and the approval she receives from them.

For some, being a workaholic stems from a different motive. This is the person who works harder and more hours than everyone else just to keep his job in a tough employment climate. He is tired, his health is failing, and he has no time for anything outside of work. But he doesn't believe he has a choice to work less because he and his family have to eat, have a place to live, and maintain the lifestyle to which they have become accustomed. He doesn't see himself as a workaholic either because he plans to cut back as soon as things get better. He might argue that he works to safeguard his financial survival.

Motive is important in this example because his motive for working is unclear. If his motive for working so hard in spite of his failing health is truly to put food on the table and a roof over his head, it might not be the result of a true other-dependent need. On the other hand, if his motivation to work to the detriment of his health, family time, leisure time, or anything else outside of work is for the approval he receives because of his sacrifice for the family, or to maintain his "bells and whistles" lifestyle, or to control the uncontrollable job situation, it is undoubtedly due to his other-dependent needs.

Although workaholics might complain about how hard they work, and they often will, each individual in the prior examples is getting something good out of satisfying their other-dependent needs, even when the end result is unhappiness. Most are so focused on satisfying their other-dependent needs that they have no time or energy left for anything or anyone else. They don't even have time to notice how unhappy they really are. They may even deny their unhappiness. On the flipside, their unhappiness is a catch-22 situation. Being a workaholic actually rewards them with approval from others for sacrificing themselves for the family, for being a dedicated and loyal worker, for the lifestyle it provides, or for being a pillar of the community. While maintaining a socially acceptable image, the workaholic can avoid unpleasant family obligations or unhappiness at home, accumulate all the bells and whistles it takes to look good to others, and enjoy being the martyr. Looking good to others and receiving approval from others may give the workaholic the illusion of happiness. However, the illusion of happiness doesn't last because it is the result of other-dependent needs.

The drawback is that workaholics have to be on the job to perpetuate the good feelings and the rewards they derive from working. Make no mistake: it's the kudos and validation, namely in the form of approval from others and their self-perceived rewards, that reinforces the continuance of the behavior.

Much like the workaholic's attempt to alleviate his or her other-dependent needs through work, there are individuals who try to satisfy their other-dependent needs in other ways. Some receive recognition and validation by being able to drink everyone else under the table or doing more drugs than their friends. Others receive approval from their peers by being recognized as the toughest member of the gang or even by committing a more heinous crime than someone else. The consequences of satisfying other-dependent needs for these individuals can be extreme. But regardless of the consequences, the price for satisfying other-dependent needs is always a greater degree of unhappiness.

The need to overcome other-dependent needs is so powerful that decent people can lose their bearings. The moral code that normally governs behavior becomes overshadowed by the overwhelming need to escape from other-dependent needs, and an unparalleled degree of unhappiness prevails.

## EXPLORATION AND DISCOVERY:

Take a look at your own other-dependent needs, i.e. the need for approval from others, looking good to others, being right, and the need to control the outcome, among others. Describe the severity of each. Compile a list of consequences you have experienced due to your other-dependent needs. Include the negative effects of each one. Do your best to look at every area of your life. Especially notice if the price of your other-dependent needs is a greater degree of unhappiness. Notice if your unhappiness has simply become normal for you. Are you trapped in a catch-22 of other-dependent needs that lead to more unhappiness, and unhappiness that leads to more other-dependent needs?

People who need to escape from the catch-22 of other-dependent needs and unhappiness often develop some unhealthy habits. These unhealthy habits are commonly referred to as addictions, which is the subject of the next chapter.

## CHAPTER SEVENTEEN

# I Don't Have an Addiction, Do I?

E ven though the goal is to escape from unhappiness, no one wants to have an addiction as defined by the dictionary—"physically dependent upon a particular substance; devoted to a particular interest or activity"—to do so.

My definition of addiction is actually the same as my definition for other-dependency: being dependent upon someone or something outside of yourself to make you feel good, or at the very least, feel better now.

Everyone who has an addiction is other-dependent. People who are other-dependent often make poor choices in an attempt to feel good. Actually all addictive behaviors are driven by the extreme need to feel good. While an addictive behavior could be one that is easily identifiable such as alcoholism, drug abuse, an eating disorder, compulsive shopping or gambling, it could be any other frequent and habitual activity that has an adverse effect upon you and your life in an attempt to feel good.

Author Anne Wilson Schaef says that we are an addictive society, supported with much evidence. If that's true, why and how does addiction happen?

You are at risk for becoming dependent upon someone or something outside yourself when you don't feel good about yourself and when you don't know how to make yourself feel better right now. Minimal or failed coping skills can lead to poor choices while trying to feel better right now. If your choice of someone or something seems to help you cope, makes you feel better, and does so quickly, it may end up becoming your favored coping method for dealing with life as it comes at you.

Some individuals depend upon a whole array of preferred coping mechanisms, often referred to as one's "drug of choice," to face all the problems, fears, stressors, or other adversities that make up life as they know it. Their dependency upon these coping mechanisms to make them feel good, or at least a little less bad, grows over time because they don't know any other way to make themselves feel better, let alone feel good—and addiction ensues.

When the only way you seem able to make yourself feel better is outside of you, you have become dependent upon those "somethings" or "someones" for the sole purpose of relief. You are other-dependent and have become addicted.

Your favored coping method can be almost anything. It can be something as innocent as working crossword puzzles, playing video games, or using your mobile phone app while walking down the sidewalk. How could these normal everyday activities be considered addictions? What is wrong with working crossword puzzles, playing video games, or using your mobile phone app? Perhaps everything is wrong or maybe nothing at all. The point here is that even the most innocent of things can become an addiction when used to escape from life as you know it in order to feel good.

The favored coping mechanism for some is literally a "drug of choice," or a medication prescribed by a physician for the sole purpose of relieving pain. For a large number of individuals, it is the repetitive use of injections designed to create a "younger-looking you." Many think there can't possibly be anything wrong with that. What can be harmful about relieving pain or creating a youthful look? After all, the prescribing physician has taken an oath to "do no harm."

For some, the favored escape mechanism might be watching hours of television every night to avoid family interaction, or to stop worrying about work, how to pay the bills, or any number of other problems. The favored escape mechanism could even be socializing on Facebook to escape for a few hours. Once again, what could possibly be wrong with that?

And then there are those whose favored coping mechanism is an external attitude presented to the world. For example, have you ever been around someone who seemed angry all the time? Or what about the "know-it-all" or someone who is always in conflict just to prove a point? Who would think the need to prove a point and be right could be considered a favored coping mechanism?

Similarly, what about the individual who takes pleasure in hurting others, either emotionally or physically? This could be his or her favored coping mechanism. It actually feels good to be mean and angry or to hurt someone because it provides this individual with an escape from his or her own painful life. Besides we all know that "misery loves company."

Whatever the favored coping mechanism, it gets used over and over again and becomes the "drug of choice" for coping, for escape, for the adrenalin rush, and ultimately for making the person feel better now or, at the very least, feel less bad.

## EXPLORATION AND DISCOVERY:

What have you used to cope with life to feel better or at least to feel less bad? Make a list. Do you have a favorite? What is it?

As you may already know, in addition to providing you with an escape route from life's problems, your favored coping mechanism can cause any number of difficulties. Just a few of the difficulties are listed here. Your favored coping mechanism can:

- make it hard to get up in the morning
- make you unhealthy and even sick
- damage relationships irreparably
- wreck you financially
- ruin your reputation
- cost you your job
- land you in jail
- destroy your life
- kill you

Even if your consequences aren't this extreme, addictive use of your favored coping mechanism always diminishes your quality of life. Your favored coping mechanism never enhances life.

**EXPLORATION AND DISCOVERY:**
How has the addictive use of your favored coping mechanism diminished your quality of life? Make a list.

Whatever your favored coping mechanism is, with all its negative consequences, it is not the real problem. Your favored coping mechanism is only a symptom of something more complex, the real problem itself.

Assuming this is accurate, what is the symptom of the problem and what is the real problem? How can you tell which is which? Let's move on to the next chapter for the answer to that question.

## CHAPTER EIGHTEEN

# What's My Problem?

*We do not see things as they are. We see things as we are.*
—The Talmud

What is the symptom of the problem and what is the real problem? How can you differentiate between the two? What **is** real and what **isn't**?

Contrary to popular belief, the real problem is neither the drugs you take nor the alcohol you drink to make yourself feel good. It is not the food you eat for comfort. Neither is it the video games, gambling, sex, or risky behaviors you engage in during your pursuit of pleasure. The real problem is not the excessive shopping, the unscrupulous accumulation of massive wealth, or the cheap and popular unhealthy fast food that you can't get enough of.

Although these addictive behaviors can cause problems by affecting lives in negative ways, they are not even close to being the problem at the heart of your lack of real and lasting happiness. None of the substances, behaviors, or activities you use to feel good will ever address or resolve the real problem because they are just symptoms *of* the real problem.

Make no mistake, the behaviors and activities you engage in to make yourself feel better, no matter how many consequences they create, will often give you the illusion of feeling good only because you feel less bad.

So what in the world *is* the real problem? **The real problem is that you have been taught to be other-dependent.** You have been taught to depend upon someone or something outside of yourself to have self-esteem, to feel good, and to be happy for real. It's sad but true that it is impossible to feel good about yourself for real when you are other-dependent. This is true no matter how much you try to make yourself believe that someone's praise, compliments, or applause, enough of the right stuff, social or financial status, an accomplishment, a success, or a Harvard degree makes you feel good about yourself. Oh sure, you may have fleeting moments of happiness here and there, but nothing that lasts. You might be able to fool yourself into thinking you feel good when your addictive behaviors distort your thinking, which they often do. You can even pretend you feel good about yourself, and you can certainly fool others, but you will always know the truth. When you don't feel good about yourself from the inside out, you don't feel good for real period. That is the real problem. Everything else is just a symptom of the real problem.

The following examples illustrate the difference between a symptom of the real problem and the real problem itself. You will see the same end result in each example: the individual is other-dependent and doesn't feel good about him or herself.

The first example has to do with an overweight individual. Let's say this person feels bad about herself because she can no longer fit into her favorite jeans, the ones that make her look "hot." She knows she will have to lose about twenty pounds to get back into those jeans. So she works hard and manages to shed that extra twenty pounds that make her feel fat. With the loss of the twenty pounds, she can get back into her favorite jeans, and she loves the way she looks in them. She feels good. But the good feeling doesn't last long. She begins once again to worry about the way she looks. Maybe those jeans really do make her look fat and not "hot" the way she thought they did. She wonders how her friends think she looks in her jeans and worries even more. The sad ending to this story is that she still feels fat and ugly even when the jeans fit. She still sees herself as a fat person and never gets to experience the joy of being at her ideal weight.

Once those extra twenty pounds were lost, you would think she should feel good about herself, especially since she looks so hot in those jeans, right? Well if she looks so hot in those jeans, why does she feel fat and ugly instead of thin and sexy? Why does she feel so self-conscious and worry about how she looks to others? Even though the extra pounds are gone, why does she still feel fat? And why does she suddenly begin to notice that her nose looks weird and that her hair is a mess? Why does she suddenly shift her focus to all the other things she thinks are wrong with her? Why does she feel uncomfortable in her own skin? Why does she begin to indulge in a little extra eating here and there again? And why does she gain back the twenty pounds, and more? If those extra pounds were the real reason for feeling bad, why didn't she continue to feel good after losing them?

In this example, she didn't feel good for very long after she lost the extra twenty pounds because the twenty pounds were not the real problem— they were only a symptom of the real problem. If the extra weight was the real problem she would continue to feel good after she lost it. Because she addressed the symptom of the problem and not the real problem, nothing changed for very long. She began eating a little extra here and there again because food is the only thing that seems to make her feel better, so she *thinks*. All she really wants is to feel good—to be happy.

The real problem in this example is that she doesn't feel good about herself and is other-dependent. She isn't happy with herself and depends upon approval from her friends to feel good. Neither gaining nor losing the extra weight will change that.

Here is another example. Let's say this person relocated to a new city because he just knew everything would be great once he got there. He knew moving to a new place was exactly what he needed to make him happy. And he was right! It was fabulous for a little while. He never felt so good. But—oh no—it didn't last. As soon as the novelty of the new place wore off, his old depressed feelings about his life resurfaced. Life didn't seem to be much different here than it was before the move. He began to notice that he didn't feel as happy anymore. It became harder than ever to get out of bed in the morning. He even started to wonder if he had made a mistake by moving. He began to think he might have been better off back where he came from. Why this change in thinking? Because moving didn't fix the real problem. If where he had been living was the real problem, he would have continued feeling happy in the new place. Moving to the new location provided a temporary distraction that seemed to make him feel good—even happy—for a little while.

Once again, in this example the place where he lived was not the real problem. Since the happiness in the new location didn't last, then it must follow that the location, old or new, was just a symptom of the real problem. When he moved, he had to take himself along too. He is other-dependent. He depends upon a particular location to make him happy. If he can't be happy in one location, he won't be happy in the next one because being happy is not about the location. When he doesn't feel good about himself and is other-dependent, he won't feel good regardless of where he is. All that really happened is that he and his problem—his other-dependency and the way he feels about himself—changed locations.

It doesn't matter where you go because once there, there you are. It doesn't matter where you live. It matters how you feel about yourself wherever you live.

Here is another example. Let's say that a woman hates her nose. It makes her feel ugly. So she gets a nose job (rhinoplasty) to make herself beautiful. Even though everyone raves about her new nose, she still feels ugly.

If her nose was truly the problem, then a perfectly beautiful new nose would fix the problem. Because she still feels ugly, even with her beautiful new nose, her nose is not the real problem. It is only a symptom of the real problem—she sees herself as ugly, with or without a beautiful nose. She is other-dependent. She is dependent upon looking good for her happiness.

Here is a final example, although there are many, many more. Let's say a man feels self-conscious whenever he attends a social event without a date or companion. He worries about what others think of him because he goes to events alone. He imagines that everyone is looking at him and thinking, *Look at that poor guy. It's too bad he had to come alone. I wonder what is wrong with him.*

Whenever he attends events alone, he has an overwhelming need to flee. His discomfort becomes so great that he vows to himself that he will not attend another social event without a companion. He gets lucky. He finds a date for the next social event. She even loves socializing. What a plus. It works. Wow! It's like magic! She makes him feel confident and secure when she is with him. He feels so good—and so happy, something he has never truly experienced before. He even likes attending social events just to show her off. And then, before he knows it, his newfound confidence begins to wane. This awesome person doesn't make him feel secure anymore. He doesn't feel as happy as he did in the beginning. Once again, he feels self-conscious socializing. What changed? The newness of this special person had begun to wear off. She wasn't quite as special as he initially thought she was. In fact, he was actually starting to wonder what people thought about his choice to be with her. What just happened?

Once again, feeling self-conscious because he was alone was not the real problem—it was only a symptom of the real problem. The new special person was only a temporary fix for the symptom of the real problem. She didn't address the real problem at all. So what is the real problem? He is other-dependent, he worries about what others think about him, and he doesn't feel good about himself whether alone or not. There isn't a single special someone on the planet outside of himself who can fix that for him.

In all of the above examples, the extra twenty pounds, a particular location, an ugly nose, and socializing without the right person were not the real problem. The real problem was that they were other-dependent: dependent on someone or something outside of themselves to feel good about themselves. The real problem of other-dependency can't be resolved by losing twenty pounds, moving to a new location, having nose surgery, or being seen with the right person. These are only temporary fixes that address the symptom. Even though changing something on the outside may work temporarily to relieve the negative, bad, or uncomfortable feelings about themselves, as long as they are other-dependent, they will never work long-term.

**EXPLORATION AND DISCOVERY:**
Make a list of some of the negative, bad, or uncomfortable feelings you have tried to fix by depending upon someone or something outside of yourself.

Most individuals engage in some kind of behavior or rely upon another person to rid themselves of their uncomfortable feelings and to make themselves feel better. In reality, most of society is doing whatever it takes on the outside to reduce feelings of inadequacy and anxiety on the inside. They are trying to create a ruse for themselves that they are as good as everyone else. Undeniably, many of these people and behaviors can have a negative effect which results in even more problems, some worse than others. Of course, you already know that.

When we don't know what the real problem is, much less how to fix it, we depend upon someone or something outside of ourselves to escape from feeling bad.

**EXPLORATION AND DISCOVERY:**
Look at your list of negative, bad, or uncomfortable feelings you have attempted to change. Now make a list of the people, places, or things you have depended upon to make you feel better. What was the result of each?
*continued...*

*...continued from previous page*

Did they work or not? What additional problems were created by them?

When we are other-dependent and see things through our lens of not being good enough instead of believing we are good enough as we are, in effect we become expert *escape artists*.

## CHAPTER NINETEEN

# The Escape Artists

The need to escape is powerful for individuals who are other-dependent and don't feel good about themselves. They often feel as though their world is falling apart or are simply waiting for something to go wrong. This need is equally as powerful for those who feel that life hasn't turned out the way it was supposed to. It is just as great for those who feel even a little bit bad from time to time. People looking for escape become extremely skilled at creating ways to avoid feeling bad. As a result, people seeking distractions are everywhere. They rely upon something or someone outside of themselves to give them a break from life—even if just for a little while.

To this end, our society is most accommodating and full of distractions. These distractions provide us with a variety of ways to escape from our own lives. These distractions can even create an illusion of being fun (we'll talk more about the difference between the illusion of fun and real fun below). Because so many of these distractions create the illusion of having fun, many individuals believe they have escaped feeling bad, no matter how short-lived. Some even have the illusion that they are getting relief from the pressures they put upon themselves to be and do better, from the stress of responsibility, from their worry about what others think about them, from real or imagined trauma, and even from their unhappiness because they aren't feeling quite so bad.

Unfortunately, the distractions can be so powerful and seductive that they might lead even the most unlikely person to participate in very extreme behaviors to escape their perceived painful life. These behaviors—which can include anything from having a few too many drinks to indiscriminate sexual encounters, cheating in a relationship, fraudulent acquisition of money, illegal drug dealing, becoming a gang member, and a variety of self-destructive activities—may compromise or destroy one's reputation, lead to a jail sentence, or result in some other very negative outcome. Risky distractions can become a matter of life and death.

It is not unusual to see examples of this in our headline news. How often is the "breaking news" about well-respected people in high places who appear to be good citizens, even the pillars of our communities, who have made poor choices in their pursuit to escape from a less than happy life? Almost daily we witness the way lives are adversely affected by this overpowering need to escape feeling bad, or, conversely, people needing to feel good, even if only for a moment. Some examples of this are athletes who choose to "dope" for a few moments of glory in the winner's circle. We see it in those who engage in extramarital affairs and/or sexual encounters for the short-lived thrill of lust and limerence (an addiction to a person that feels like love but isn't). And what about the loss of reputation and even the loss of life for countless celebrities who turn to alcohol and drugs to escape?

Even individuals who don't make "breaking news" but also need to escape pain, whether physical or emotional, are usually decent people—outwardly hardworking, respected members of society. They may be a friend or neighbor whose overpowering need to escape has led them to make some very poor choices.

For some escape artists the drugs, alcohol, sex, chocolate cake, or whatever is strictly used as the mechanism to numb out. What about that little glass of wine or two or more that some individuals look forward to after a stressful day at work? Isn't it interesting that for many, feeling nothing feels better than the feelings they are used to having? Essentially, for them, feeling nothing is equal to feeling good. Not feeling anything feels better than feeling something. They must feel good since they're not feeling anything at all, they reason.

**EXPLORATION AND DISCOVERY:**

What poor and perhaps self-destructive choices have you made to escape feeling bad? For example, when did you eat a whole bag of chips while watching your favorite television program, or spend part of the rent money to buy something you just had to have, or downed too many drinks even though you had plans with family or friends? How about being flirtatious with the boss or a coworker for attention, compromising your safety or reputation just to be a part of the group, or even yelling in front of everyone just to make a point? Make a list.

It has become quite normal today for many individuals to abuse alcohol because it's such a quick and easy way to escape. However, some people abuse alcohol and/or drugs for a different reason. It can provide them with a guilt-free way to escape their perceived responsibilities and obligations. Being high or intoxicated is a perfect excuse to do nothing for someone who is lazy—it's a guilt-free way to take a timeout from worrying about what others think about them.

On the other hand there are people who must always be doing something. They just can't do nothing even when they have nothing to do. For them, their to-do list is a trap and being drunk or high is the only way they can comfortably justify taking a break.

For both the lazy person and the busy person, being drunk or high gives them a pass from what others might think of them. After all, others can't expect too much from them when they're drunk, can they? No need to worry that they should be cleaning the house or washing the car when they're high on drugs. No need to worry about what others might be thinking at all—not when they're drunk or high. And it's easy to justify. Everyone they know gets drunk or a little high every once in a while.

Then there's the individual who doesn't find drinking an acceptable behavior at all—let alone getting high on drugs. What options are available to this person to escape for a little while? Believe it or not, the options are numerous.

There is the individual who "lives to eat." This person doesn't do any of those obviously bad things. Eating food, even too much of it, is easy to justify. After all, everyone has to eat. You need food to stay alive, don't you? And what about the person who gets lost in the pages of a good book to the neglect of everything else? It's a great way to escape without doing anything wrong—and again so easy to justify.

Even the person who suffers from depression may use it as a great excuse to escape. This is not intended to trivialize severe depression in any way. But for many, depression is an acceptable and legitimate way to do nothing. They can stay in bed and pull the covers up over their heads. And it's just as easy to justify as any of the more obvious methods of escape.

**EXPLORATION AND DISCOVERY:**
Have you thought of any other escape mechanisms you use that seem socially acceptable? How do you justify your escape mechanism of choice?

People who value themselves don't hurt themselves with destructive escape mechanisms and don't have to make excuses for doing nothing. People who value themselves give themselves permission to relax and do nothing at all. And they give themselves permission to participate in fun, playful, even frivolous activities. One of my clients, George, says, "When you have nothing to do, take the time to do nothing."

Make no mistake: escape is not fun and fun is not escape. Fun and escape in the same sentence is an oxymoron. The purpose of escape is to get rid of something undesirable. There is nothing fun about having to depend upon something or someone to escape from feeling bad—especially if it makes you numb or puts your life in danger.

Conversely, fun is experienced with every one of your senses. You have to be present to have fun. You can't be numb and truly experience fun. It requires a particular mindset. You can even have fun all by yourself while doing nothing at all!

For example, a woman I know depended upon compulsive reading as a child to escape painful family and social experiences. This highly sensitive person would lose herself in a safe world as an observer, where nothing could directly hurt her, and yet it became addictive because she was experiencing the emotional connection she craved in the real world vicariously through the safety of the characters in her books.

## EXPLORATION AND DISCOVERY:

Give yourself permission to have real fun. You may choose to do something you think is fun, playful, or even frivolous. Or you may choose to think yourself into having fun while doing nothing at all. Remember, thinking makes it so. You may not utilize whatever you have done in the past to escape. Write about your experience. If you don't have fun doing what you have chosen to do, you don't have to do it again, but you won't know if it is fun or not until you do it.

Since we haven't been taught how to have fun beyond the experience of our childhood fun, most of us have become dependent upon some kind of substitute for fun. These substitutes have normalized the abnormal in our attempt to escape from feeling bad. Let's move on to the next chapter to explore this new normal.

## CHAPTER TWENTY

# The New Normal

Because so many individuals have a great need to escape real life due to other-dependency, abnormal and even unthinkable behaviors have become the new normal in our society.

Of course, heading up the list is the overuse of alcohol. It is considered normal to drink more than a beer or two after work or celebrate happy hour with more than a few drinks. It has become fairly normal protocol to wrap up an important business deal over drinks, with or without dinner.

Likewise, it is considered normal to pick up a six-pack—and not of soda pop—at the local convenience store after work and drink all six in front of the television—and the kids—before falling asleep. And what about the person who thinks it is perfectly normal to routinely have a couple glasses of wine while preparing dinner, just to unwind after a day at work or a day with the kids? Some find it impossible to have a good steak without the perfect wine to go with it. Others consider it normal to celebrate weekends drinking at the clubs to meet people and have a little fun. Thousands of sports fans are unable to attend a sporting event or watch a Sunday afternoon or Monday night football game without a few beers—sometimes so many beers they don't even know who won when the game is over. For some, a couple of arrests for driving while intoxicated has become the new normal—even a few days in jail is no big deal.

In fact, these practices have become so normal that 52 percent of society is considered to be "regular drinkers" and 23 percent are "binge drinkers."[1] The Centers for Disease Control considers a "regular drinker" to be someone who has twelve drinks over the course of one year. It defines "binge drinking" as five or more drinks for men and four or more drinks for women over a period of two hours and a pattern of drinking that results in a blood alcohol concentration of 0.08 grams or above.[2] Drinking has become so normal that in some circles it is even thought that there is something wrong with the person who doesn't drink alcohol at all.

Drugs, legal or illegal, are another example of the new normal. Why do Americans toke 25 million marijuana joints each year?[3] It is becoming increasingly normal for people to smoke a joint at night to relax after a stressful day. Some even grow their own marijuana to avoid the cost of buying and the risk associated with drug dealers. Celebrities who have been in and out of rehab routinely defend their medical use of marijuana by denying their addiction to this addictive drug.

And just why do Americans take one million tablets of Ecstasy each year?[4]

Perhaps the most dangerous of all is the legal prescription drug consumption that is destroying family systems and claiming an excessive number of lives due to overdose. For example, one person dies every nineteen minutes from a drug overdose.[5] The prescription painkiller Oxycodone was the leading cause of drug-related deaths in Florida in 2008.[6] This has become the new normal among young and old alike.

As a result of this new normal, many individuals have become alcoholics and/or drug addicts without knowing it because they think their routine of often daily use is perfectly normal. After all, everyone they know has a few beers, a glass of wine, a couple of cocktails, smokes a "little weed," and/or is on some kind of prescribed medication. It's the normal thing to do. Similarly, consider the politicians, celebrities, and athletes who find it quite normal to have a drink and/or joint before and/or after a political rally, theatrical performance, or strenuous athletic competition. And what about the athlete who defends having a beer during the competition as something any normal person would do?

Of course, celebrities aren't the only people filling up the beds and patient lists in treatment programs, detox facilities, and rehabilitation centers. They're full to the rafters with our neighbors, our family members, our coworkers, and every other kind of everyday person you can think of. Maybe you've even been there yourself.

Unfortunately, alcohol and drug use is not the only characteristic of the new normal. Doesn't everyone eat fast food? Why do Americans consume 40 million pounds of chocolate and 400,000 tons of sugar each year? Why do millions of people overeat every day? Why are there 12 million overweight kids in this country? Why has it become necessary to develop statin drugs for 9-year-olds who already have high cholesterol?

What about all the less obvious new-normal behaviors? For example, the individual who moves across the country to a new location for no particular reason other than everything will be better there? What about the person who has multiple extramarital affairs for love or sex? What about those who engage in unprotected sex or masturbate numerous times daily?

Have you ever noticed that every time you turn on the television or open the pages of a magazine, you see ads for depression or anxiety medications? Why do Americans swallow 20 million antidepressants and smoke 8.25 billion cigarettes every year? What about those who continue to smoke cigarettes even while on life support?

Why did the typical American watch an average of 34 hours of television per week in 2010?[7] Likewise, why has the world spent the equivalent of 200,000 years playing the game Angry Birds?[8]

While the numbers I've just cited continue to increase, we could add statistics for many other new-normal behaviors. Look at how normal it has become for both parents to work 24/7 to get ahead while the children fend for themselves. What about the person whose motto is "shop until you drop"? The ease of "charging it" is another new normal for those who don't have cash. We could add the growing number of people who go into debt every year because of gambling and overspending as well as the 10 percent of Americans who shoplift to feel better.[9]

Of course, once we engage in any of the new-normal behaviors, we have to make it okay to continue doing so by minimizing, rationalizing, and justifying them, not only to others but to ourselves. We say things like "Everyone I know is doing it" or "I'm not as bad about it as my friends" or "I only do it every once in a while" or "I'm not hurting anyone" or "I'm doing it for my family." Approval from others makes it even easier to continue our new-normal behaviors. This is even seen in the case of individuals who are intent upon supersized breasts, skin-tightening procedures, anti-wrinkle and lip plumping chemical injections (commonly referred to as "trout pout"), and cosmetic surgery on any "unacceptable" body part.

**EXPLORATION AND DISCOVERY:**
What abnormal behaviors have you normalized for yourself without realizing it? How do you minimize, rationalize, and justify engaging in them to others? How do you minimize, rationalize, and justify engaging in them to yourself?

The results of the new-normal are quite startling. The number of highly respected individuals who experience the loss of reputation is rapidly increasing. Our divorce rate is the highest ever. Obesity is out of control. High school dropout rates are soaring. Loss of employment is at an all-time high. Financial difficulties are on the rise.

For some, even the consequences of the new-normal behaviors have become a new-normal. Jails and prisons are constantly overcrowded due to alcohol- and drug-related crimes committed by very good people who have engaged in the new-normal. Being arrested for "driving under the influence"

(DUI), disorderly conduct, public intoxication, possession of marijuana and other illegal drugs, alcohol- and drug-related domestic battery, even mass shootings and other violent crimes have all become new-normals for much of society. According to the most recent data available, 760 per 100,000 people are in prison or jail in the United States—that means 7.1 million individuals are incarcerated![10] One in every 132 people is behind bars.[11] This rate is more than 3 times higher than the country with the next-highest incarceration rate, Poland, which has a rate of 224 per 100,000 people, while the lowest incarceration rate belongs to Iceland, with a rate of 44 per 100,000.[12] In 1980, the number of people incarcerated in the United States was one quarter of what it is now. The dramatic increase has been attributed to the war on drugs. As you can see, no other country comes close to our rate of incarceration, and prisons are big business.[13]

**EXPLORATION AND DISCOVERY:**
What are the results and/or consequences of your own new-normal behaviors? Make a list.

You might be wondering what is abnormal about having a few too many drinks with friends to relax or indulging in a little too much chocolate once in a while or even spending more money than you make. What's new about that? Doesn't everyone want the best education at the most prestigious Ivy League school? Who doesn't want to work harder than everyone else in order to shop more, buy more, save more, and have more? It isn't abnormal to work hard. People have been working hard for centuries. What could possibly be wrong with a move across country? Everyone is on the move these days. What could possibly be abnormal about that? Perhaps nothing and maybe everything. It all depends upon your motive! Is your motive to make yourself happy?

## EXPLORATION AND DISCOVERY:

Make a list of the new-normal activities you engage in and your motive for doing them. What are your reasons for doing what you do? Are you able to recognize your other-dependency? Do you recognize your attempt to make yourself happy?

Here is another perspective on the new-normals. There once was a time when being the "town drunk" was not the norm. Now it's normal to be "drunk on the town." There was a time when fast food wasn't the norm either. Up until 1940 there was no place to buy fast food. McDonald's hadn't yet been built and it wasn't franchised until 1955. You had to purchase your food in a market, or grow your own and prepare it. There was a time when it wasn't even possible to shop 24/7, let alone normal—no matter how hard you worked or how much money you had. Very few retail stores, if any in some communities, were open after 5 p.m. and certainly not on Sunday. There was no Internet and therefore no Amazon.com. There was no QVC, Home Shopping Network, or other shopping networks on television for your shopping convenience. You couldn't stay home and shop in your pajamas. You had to get up out of your chair, get dressed, and go to the store during a limited number of hours to make your purchase.

Similarly, it was not normal to move across country away from the family just on a lark or even for a better job. Other new-normals didn't yet exist. For example, there was nothing normal about playing Angry Birds, tweeting, or spending every spare moment on Facebook because these options were not available prior to the twenty-first century. Today's standards for normal have drastically changed from yesterday's normal. What was considered to be abnormal just a few years ago has been normalized. Why? The mechanism that compels respectable people to normalize abnormal behaviors is *other-dependency*. Respectable people have normalized abnormal behaviors in the pursuit of real happiness.

### EXPLORATION AND DISCOVERY:

Do your best to identify the abnormal behaviors you have normalized in your pursuit of real happiness. You may not have realized prior to right now that you were engaging in these abnormal behaviors just to make yourself feel good. Once again, see if you can recognize why you have been engaging in these abnormal behaviors. What was your motive? Was it instant gratification? For clarity, these abnormal behaviors do not include an occasional fast-food meal or the moderate use of Facebook.

Let's take a look at how our need for instant gratification affects the choices we make on a daily basis in the next chapter.

# The Feel-Good-Now Syndrome

The desire to feel good is within all of us. It is so powerful that it has become the driving force of almost everyone on the planet. Although not everyone needs the same thing to make them feel good, the need is so powerful for some individuals that they are willing to risk everything, even death, for only a few fleeting moments of feeling good and feeling good NOW.

The need to feel good now has become so powerful that we are a feel-good-now society whose present and rising generation is known as the "Now Generation." An attitude of "I want to feel good, and I want to feel good now" prevails. There is no place in this type of attitude for delayed gratification—not when you can have it now.

Due to this mindset, not only do many individuals depend upon someone or something outside of themselves to make them feel good, they want whatever it is they are dependent upon to make them feel good instantly.

As previously discussed, drugs and alcohol may head up the list of obvious things people use to make themselves feel good quickly, but the list extends far beyond these substances. Fast food, particularly in the United States, is a top contender. For many, hunger creates the need to feel better right now. Fast food is a quick-fix for being hungry and a fast food drive-thru is even quicker. You don't even have to dress for the occasion; you can stay in your bathrobe. Consequently, fast food has become the means of instant gratification used by millions as a quick-fix for the need to feel good now. It doesn't matter that it is not nutritious. It also doesn't matter that it is usually loaded with empty calories. The only thing that does matter is that it fulfills the need to feel good instantly without having to do anything for it—no need to plant the seeds, grow the food, harvest it, or prepare it. Just pick it up, eat it, and feel good now. And if your choice of food gives you indigestion—well, there's a pill to fix that just as fast.

According to a new study even the quantity and size of the fast food quick-fix meal matters to individuals with low incomes. Relatively cheap supersized portions and lots of them seem to temporarily give people a powerful boost in self-importance.[14] It makes them feel good now.

Fast food chains aren't the only successful businesses benefitting from our obsession with food to make us feel good now. Books about food, new and better diets, and healthy eating are introduced into the marketplace almost daily. Weight loss programs thrive as a direct result of our dependency upon food to make us feel good. When diets and weight loss programs aren't fast enough we go in search of a pill that will do the work for us. And when all else fails, which it usually does, stomach bypass surgery rises to the top of the quick-fix weight loss list. Likewise, the majority of physicians' waiting rooms are packed with unhealthy people who have a myriad of ailments as a result of unhealthy eating habits.

Similarly, what about those who want that new car, house, or "fill-in-the-blank"—and want it now? They give little or no thought about how to pay for the desired object. So what if their credit cards will be maxed out and the payments are more than they can afford? They can simply worry about that later. It really doesn't matter right now because having what they want and having it now makes them feel good now.

**EXPLORATION AND DISCOVERY:**
What can't you do without? What do you need to make yourself feel good now? Make a list.

Another example of the need to feel good now is the individual who experiences pain, either physical or emotional. The need to feel good right away can be so strong that individuals of all ages get blindsided by it. No matter that relief, many times in the form of prescription medications, seldom fixes the root cause of the pain, nor does it fix unhappiness. It doesn't even seem to matter that millions of individuals become addicted to these prescribed medications, many overdosing and dying, just to make their pain go away so they can have the illusion of feeling good immediately. There is no happiness attached to this kind of feeling good.

For clarity, besides the many people who overmedicate and get into serious trouble with pain medications of all types, there are people with chronic illnesses who don't want to take medications. They never abuse them but take them just to function. Yet for most there is no happiness attached to this way of life either. In fact, this is an example of how thinking, when implemented with focused intent, can create a shift to inner happiness *despite* chronic illness and/or pain. Methods to achieve real happiness in spite of physical or emotional pain will be discussed in greater detail in future chapters. However, you can begin to make a shift to happiness by engaging in the following *Exploration and Discovery* exercise.

**EXPLORATION AND DISCOVERY:**

If you experience emotional or physical pain, I want you to focus on anything and everything you currently have to be grateful for. Perhaps someone special who provides love and care for you, a good neighbor, a pet, a bed to sleep in, food to eat, a good book to read, a favorite television show to watch, a rainy day, a sunny day, the fact that you are alive. Nothing is too big or too small to put on your list. Start making your list now.

Regardless of your personal experience, the need to feel good now provides the fuel to engage in the new-normal activities and behaviors. Yet even though "everyone else" seems to be doing them, the majority of individuals who engage in these activities and behaviors don't want to be found out. They don't want to get caught doing what they're doing. Some experience a sense of shame on the inside because of their heart/ conscience speaking up, even if they may not understand why. For example, something as innocuous as playing a game app on their phone can be used as a way to escape. And even though they think everyone does it, they may still want to do it in secret when they use it to escape. As a result, they end up with a lot of secrets. These secrets are the perfect formula for becoming the *Great Pretender.*

# The Great Pretenders

The Great Pretenders all have secrets. Anyone who tries to hide anything about themselves from others becomes an expert at pretending. People who lack self-esteem go to great lengths to hide their self-perceived flaws and faults. They don't want others to know about their poor choices, mistakes, and failures. You know what I'm talking about—hiding the things you don't want anyone to know about you for fear they'll think you're weird, won't like you, won't want to be around you, or might be disappointed in you. It's these things you try to keep hidden from others that become your secrets.

As a result of all this pretending, people become as "sick as their secrets." What does this mean? It means that pretenders almost always ends up feeling bad about themselves because hiding a secret becomes an open wound that festers. The secret is the infection. If you ask some of the greatest pretenders how they are, they will be quick to tell you how great they feel. They believe they have to behave as if they have nothing to hide or they'll blow their cover. They don't want to blow their fake façade because they need to look good to others. However, they quite often become emotional train-wrecks on the inside because of their constant effort to look cool on the outside while keeping their secrets hidden from others. It takes a lot of mental and emotional energy to stay on top of their secrets.

These individuals pretend that whatever it is they are hiding doesn't exist in order to feel safe. They often choose to outright lie to others. At other times they lie by omission and then try to justify the omission by convincing themselves that "what you don't know won't hurt you." An excellent example of lying by omission occurs when children keep secrets from their parents. They do so not only for fear of being in trouble, but for a much bigger reason: not wanting to disappoint them and not wanting to lose their approval.

Either way, people with secrets, whether young or old, fear that if their secrets are revealed to others they will be exposed for who and what they really are. They generally feel like fakes. They are almost always "looking over their shoulder" in fear of being found out. These secrets contribute to their inability to ever let their guard down, which makes it impossible for them to relax. Anxiety is a common feeling for the great pretenders.

The secrets people pretend don't exist vary from person to person. They can be real or imagined. They can be big or little. Secrets can be anything—where you were born and to whom, childhood teasing, flunking kindergarten, losing a competition, being chosen last for sides on a team event, having a teenage sexual encounter, being unpopular in school, saying something stupid when you were trying to impress someone, growing up poor, a bounced check, dropping out of college, being fired from a job, or any one of a thousand other things that made you feel inferior as a person. Some people might think it is ridiculous to worry about hiding secrets like these. What's the big deal?

The big deal for the great pretenders is that they have to keep their secrets hidden because they are worried about what others think about them. Conversely, there are those who are hiding much bigger secrets: out-of-control anger, violent behaviors, dishonesty, gang membership, illegal drug use, or other criminal activity.

There are all kinds of people with all kinds of secrets. The list of secrets is endless. And no matter how big or small, they are very real. Whatever is on your list of secrets can be traumatic and emotionally debilitating. These secrets are the direct result of a negative self-perception and self-deprecation that end up in self-victimization.

**EXPLORATION AND DISCOVERY:**

Is there anything you are trying to hide about yourself? Can you identify any of your secrets? Write them all down—don't leave any out. What are you afraid of? What do you fear other people might find out about you? Be brutally honest with yourself as you make your list.

The Great Pretenders have a real need to be just like everyone else. This is another reason why they don't want anyone to know about the things they try to keep hidden. They often feel different from others because of their secrets. They are usually uncomfortable with themselves while trying to be the same as everyone else.

What the Great Pretenders don't realize is that almost everyone has a secret of some kind. So while the pretenders are trying to be just like everyone else, everyone else is trying to be just like them. You feel insecure and so do they. Their pretending comes from the same source as yours—you fear that you might not look good or be right, and you fear what others might think about you.

In contrast to the Great Pretenders, who are trying to be like everyone else, there are those who have given up on that idea. They are equally uncomfortable with themselves; they just pretend differently. These individuals are loud and obnoxious. They may display socially unacceptable behavior and feel proud about the way they act. They use this behavior as a protective smokescreen to keep others from glimpsing their hidden secrets. And just in case there is any doubt that they are okay, their bravado proves they are. They create an aura of unshakeable self-confidence. They try to show everyone that they've "got it all going on." They do this to garner admiration from others. They have become the "Greatest Pretenders" of all because their bravado is usually far from what is real for them.

And then there are those who find it easier to be as "glib" as everyone else when they are intoxicated from alcohol or high on drugs. Their secret is that they need to feel buzzed to comfortably socialize with others—to be able to speak with as much ease as everyone else seems to do. Alcohol hasn't earned the nickname "liquid courage" for no reason.

Others might find it easier to pretend to be cool while safely hiding in cyberspace through Facebook or Twitter interactions. A total "pretend" persona can be manufactured online. You can become anyone you want to be. It's that easy. There are some who will engage in Internet pornography or telephone sex to pretend they are sexy or desirable. Of course, this only creates more secrets to pretend don't exist.

Go to www.goodwithme.com/resources for your free in-depth article titled "Looking Good on Facebook."

Still others completely opt out socially. They don't even try to pretend. They just want to be left alone, even making excuses to do so. In solitude they can eat the whole box of chocolates, the whole bag of chips, or even drink the whole bottle of alcohol all by themselves. For them it is just too hard to try to pretend to hide from their secrets.

Whatever your reason for pretending that your secret doesn't exist— and you know what it is—it doesn't change anything. Think about it this way. You might be able to hide your secret from others but you can't hide it from yourself.

While pretending that your secret doesn't exist, you may engage in behaviors or use substances that create even more secrets for you to hide. You just end up creating more reasons to feel even worse. It becomes a never-ending cycle, and the negative effects accumulate. The secrets get bigger and bigger, and they become harder to hide.

Many begin lying to family and friends to cover up their secret. Some will drink or drug more than ever. Others will start eating junk food and putting on extra pounds. Most live in constant fear that someone will find out about their secret—whatever it is. They may begin to miss more work than they can afford to miss and still keep their job. They may ignore the bills that pile up. They may even begin to isolate from society. It takes more and more energy to keep their secret hidden.

### EXPLORATION AND DISCOVERY:

What have you done to try to keep your secret a secret? How much energy has it taken to do so? How bad are the negative effects of trying to hide it?

For most people, pretending eventually fails. You undoubtedly already know that engaging in unhealthy behaviors to hide your secrets creates even bigger secrets that are more difficult to hide. Pretending becomes a downward spiral to nowhere. So now what?

It's time for you to learn what I've learned and others have learned. It's time to learn that it's okay to make poor choices and mistakes and that it's okay to fail. It's time to learn that poor choices and mistakes are not failures. Instead, you are learning how to succeed. That's when you can finally stop hiding. You can finally stop being fake and phony. The Great Pretenders keep secrets because they fear being different. When you give yourself permission to be different you can finally stop pretending!

Let's move on to the next chapter to learn more about how to overcome your fears of being different.

# Different Just Like You

Are you afraid to be different because you worry about what others will think of you? Does your need to look good to others prevent you from being who you really are? People who are other-dependent are constantly comparing themselves to others to figure out how they should or shouldn't be. They are afraid to be different for fear of disapproval from others.

Much of the foundation that makes it okay to be different, specifically our self-esteem, has been established by the time we are five or six years of age. Numerous studies indicate that our self-esteem doesn't change very much by the time we become teenagers. Unfortunately, what these numerous studies don't understand is that most of us have been taught to have other-dependent esteem instead of self-dependent esteem. These studies pay little, if any, attention to the idea that it is actually our dependency upon what others think of us that doesn't change very much. Because of this dependency upon what others think about us, especially our peers, it doesn't feel good to be different. In fact, for most teenagers it's much too frightening.

As teenagers we are faced with the difficulties created by our dependency upon what others think about us at the very time we are seeking to create our own identity and become independent. We begin to have our own ideas, often separate from our parents' ideas about life—even though we are still substantially dependent upon our parents. This struggle between dependency and the feeling that our parents don't know what they are talking about (or that they are impossible to please) leads us to look for likeminded individuals. We look to our peers to find someone who is different just like us. We look to these peers for support, even when it might not be good for us.

Some of us are very selective about the particular person or group we choose to emulate and others of us will lower our standards to be different like our chosen group. For most of us though, the only way being different is safe is when being different isn't really being different. As a result, our mantra during the teen years and beyond is "I want to be different JUST LIKE YOU."

### EXPLORATION AND DISCOVERY:

Have you ever admired a particular person or group of people who were different and chose to be different just like them? See if you can identify who that was. What were the results?

The struggles and tug-of-war between teens and parents often lead to teen rebellion. During this time of rebellion, the teen is essentially telling the parent, "I'll show you; I'll hurt me." In other words, "I'll hurt you by hurting myself." This rebellious attitude can often lead to some outrageous behaviors on the part of the teenager.

For many, this struggle continues into adulthood. Believe it or not, adults rebel too. Parents are replaced by any and all authority figures—even the establishment and the rules of society in general. Their motto is "no one is going to tell me what to do." Their teenage rebellion against a parent's controlling behavior has continued into adulthood and they are still saying "I'll show you; I'll hurt me."

Just like teenagers, these adults look for likeminded adults. They still want to be different (that is, special and unique), even while they continue to look for a place where others think good thoughts about them. It appears that even as adults most have not figured out that there is nothing wrong or bad about being different from others in the sense that they are more or less pretty, handsome, educated, wealthy, popular, or just different from others due to their life experience. Or they see themselves lacking when compared to their admired group or superstar. It is this subtle difference that often feels wrong.

Some examples of being different are listed below.

- I struggle with my grades and you don't.
- I don't score as many points as the rest of the team.
- My verbal skills are not as good as yours.
- I am not as artistic as my friend.
- I don't have the gift of gab like you.
- My wardrobe came from a consignment shop.
- I am a geek.
- I love opera.
- I am a perfectionist.
- I speak several foreign languages.
- I am a great conversationalist.
- I am a superstar rock singer.
- I am a great quarterback.
- I am drop-dead gorgeous.

It doesn't matter how you are different to think that it is wrong or bad. Of course, being different is neither wrong nor bad. Being different is just being different.

Those who bully and those who allow themselves to be bullied present another example of the way different is considered to be wrong. For example, if I think you are smarter and prettier than I am, I am jealous and envious of you. I feel different from you, but more importantly, I feel less than you. I seek approval from my group of friends by taking you down a notch or two. I feel good when I make you look stupid. Or, just the opposite, I think you are dumber and dorkier than I am. I don't like you because you are weird. I don't want to be like you either. I think I look good to others when I pick on you and make you wrong for being so different.

In these examples the bully sees himself as different and not good enough, and so does the bullied. The bullied allows himself to be bullied because he feels different and being different feels bad.

Go to www.goodwithme.com/resources for an in-depth article on bullying titled "The Bully and the Bullied."

## EXPLORATION AND DISCOVERY:

How important is it to you to be different just like your chosen group? Do you feel something is wrong with you because you are different from others? How are you different from others? What are the good points about being different from others? Write about it.

Just as most of us have been taught to be other-dependent, similarly most of us have been taught that there is something wrong or bad about being different. Even when we are told it's okay to be different, we don't really believe it because of the way society responds to being different.

Here is a sampling of how much of society around the world responds to being different.

Example 1: Your skin color is different from mine. You are bad.

Example 2: Your beliefs are different from mine. You are wrong.

Example 3: Your government is different from ours. You are bad and wrong.

### EXPLORATION AND DISCOVERY:

Can you add some of your own ideas and societal conditioning to this list? Write them down here.

Here is some food for thought. We all have different life experiences. Everyone doesn't see life through the same lens. When you disparage others because they are different from you, it isn't because there is something wrong with them. You may think there is something wrong with them because you are not okay with yourself. The reality is that we judge others to the degree we judge ourselves. We criticize others to the extent we criticize ourselves. Different is wrong and bad for those who are other-dependent.

Dr. Wayne W. Dyer, internationally renowned author and speaker, says, "When you judge another, you do not define them, you define yourself."

Contrary to different being wrong or bad, some people view being different as a good thing. When individuals think they are better than others because of their differences, their mantra is: "I am different because I am better than you." They may think they are better than you because they have more money, more intelligence, more talent, more social status, or more of anything. They don't need to be different just like you; they don't even want to be like you because they think they are better than you.

This is just a smokescreen to convince themselves and others that they are better than everyone else and it is okay to be "their kind of different." This is actually another example of being dependent upon what others think. This individual is still trying to be different just like their chosen group of peers who see themselves as better than others.

An example of this kind of different is the perfectionist who believes she is different and better than most people. It is the honor roll student who makes the Dean's List with a 4.0+ grade point average who sees himself as different and better than his peers.

**EXPLORATION AND DISCOVERY:**

Do you need to be more and have more than others to convince yourself that you are better than others? Do you believe that "your kind of different" makes you better than others?

Then there are the loners who are different just like no one else. They are so different that others avoid being around them. Being different for the loners can be quite painful. They have given up on being like anyone.

They say they have given up on caring what their peers think about them. They believe they have been let down by others. These individuals hate the idea that they might have to depend upon anyone outside of themselves to meet their needs. Their mantra is: "No thank you. I can do it all by myself. I don't need your help. I'll show you!" This is often someone who has no self-dependent esteem and no other-dependent esteem either. They may rebel against everyone in society so vehemently that their rebellion can become violent. Some will even rebel against themselves.

Despite our fear of being different, different actually can be good. You may be different from someone else, but that doesn't mean there's something wrong with you. It doesn't mean you are bad. You might look different, know different information, be good at different things, have a different job, live in a different neighborhood, have been born into a different race, have a different sexual orientation or different religious beliefs, but different is simply different. Besides, it would serve no useful purpose if everyone on the planet was exactly the same. That would be boring. As human beings, we may never totally stop comparing ourselves to others, but we can stop denigrating or degrading ourselves for being different. Then and only then can we let go of our fear of being different and accept that different is simply different.

In the final analysis, people who fear being different have a need to fit in and belong somewhere, somehow. Let's explore what happens to individuals who need to fit in and belong in the next chapter.

# Get in Where You Fit In

Fitting in and belonging somewhere, somehow, is the goal for people who are afraid to be different. Individuals who have no real identity of their own find that being part of a group is the perfect fit for them because the group provides them with an identity. The need to fit in and belong is overwhelmingly powerful and important to those who are other-dependent, regardless of gender, age, color, race, culture, or religion.

The types of available groups where one can fit in and belong are unlimited. All you have to do to get in where you fit in is to think like the group. Fitting in, whether it's joining a sorority or fraternity, a country club, an art club, a martial arts group, an Alcoholics Anonymous group, a biker's group, a street gang, or a cult, is an important priority for those who are dependent upon the approval and acceptance of others to feel okay.

Fitting in and belonging to a group can be a great source of other-dependent esteem for the group members. The other-dependent esteem provided by the group can feel just like self-dependent esteem. There is a difference though. Other-dependent esteem belongs to the group while self-dependent esteem belongs to you. Other-dependent esteem provided by the group is temporary and will be gone when the group is gone. Self-dependent esteem belongs to you and is yours to keep.

Unfortunately for some, it doesn't matter what the group stands for or what their values are. They simply take on the identity provided for them by the group and often do so without question. It doesn't even matter if it ruins their reputation. Just being a group member and fitting in is enough. Group members will often make the necessary adjustments to fit in even if the adjustments they make go against their own personal values. The need to fit in and belong can be so strong that one's own personal values are tossed aside and are no longer of any importance.

The standard for fitting in with certain groups may be considerably lower than others even though quite costly. The student who receives a school suspension for smoking dope behind the fence with the cool group is an illustration of this. Likewise, the individual who goes to happy hour every day after work with coworkers instead of going home for dinner with the family may pay a heavy price for the need to fit in and belong. Not only is the family relationship in jeopardy, but what about the potential loss of employment for coming in to work day after day with an obvious hangover?

Similarly there are a myriad of consequences for the individual who parties at the clubs all weekend just to fit in and belong to a cool group of friends. And what about those who pierce their tongues and other body parts or cover their entire bodies with tattoos to fit in? Not only is there no guarantee the person who wants to fit in will continue to like their piercings and tattoos later in life, there is also no guarantee the group will accept this person as a member.

Some individuals are willing to risk everything meaningful to them because being part of a group means they are no longer alone. They find power and strength in numbers. The "just follow the crowd" mentality sets in.

**EXPLORATION AND DISCOVERY:**
What have you been willing to risk just to fit in and belong? What price have you been willing to pay in order to fit in and belong?

For some, the stakes are exceptionally high. They will do whatever it takes, behave in any manner, and even participate in risky activities to be recognized by their selected peer group. Some individuals will put themselves into great financial difficulty just to fit in and belong at whatever they have chosen, whether it be joining a club, having political ambitions, or riding the biggest Harley. They will often go deeply into debt to be seen with the right things in the right places with the right people.

There are those who are willing to engage in immoral and/or illegal behaviors to have a sense of belonging. What about the individual who participates in a criminal activity, in spite of their morals and values, just to fit in? The price of fitting in doesn't matter because the only thing that has any importance is satisfying the need to belong. We see the manifestations of this need in the news every day. Someone is always making the headlines for this very reason—the need to fit in and belong.

Even influential and wealthy individuals sacrifice a great deal to fit in. The "Ponzi Schemers" are one example of this need to fit in and belong to an elite group. Athletes who allegedly dope to win competitions are another example. Why would these people who seem to have it all jeopardize so much to belong to their chosen group of elitists? That's the power of the need to fit in.

**EXPLORATION AND DISCOVERY:**
What have you jeopardized in order to fit in and belong? What consequences have you experienced due to your choice to do whatever it takes to fit in and belong? Write about it.

The behaviors chosen by some individuals to fit in and belong don't necessarily have to be mischievous or illegal. For example, as a teenager you might have dropped out of school and spent all your time connecting with other dropouts on Facebook to fit in and belong. Or you might have worked at a part-time job so you could fit in with the crème de la crème group by wearing only the most expensive, trendy designer clothes and owning all the latest electronic gadgets. You might have practiced hour after endless hour in athletics to be a star athlete so you could fit in with the popular sports jocks.

**EXPLORATION AND DISCOVERY:**
Make a list of the choices you made as a teenager to fit in and belong. The following narrative may be helpful to you in figuring this out for yourself.

"I was a straight-A student. I had to do well academically because of my parents' influence. They graduated from Harvard, and it was expected that I would do the same. I knew I'd be accepted; after all, maintaining a 4.0 and higher was easy. Everyone at school thought I was really smart, and for a while I felt proud of my grades. But I didn't much like being called nerd and geek by some of my classmates. It hurt that I was never invited to any of the cool parties. I felt as if I stood out like a sore thumb with those honor roll grades, so I disregarded my parents' hope that I would follow in their footsteps and make something of myself.

"I started to let my grades slip—I actually had to dumb-down so that I could fit in and belong. I finally quit doing my homework and sometimes even skipped a class here and there. I smoked a little pot once in a while, even though I hated the way it made me feel. I wanted to belong to the cool group so much that it no longer mattered that my parents were very disappointed in what happened to my grades and that they were worried about what was happening to me. They couldn't figure out why I had all of a sudden lost my honors grade point average. They were shocked when I was given a three-day suspension from school for smoking weed. They couldn't figure out what had happened to me. It felt awful to disappoint them, but I tried to ignore those feelings and did my best to avoid my parents as much as possible. I wanted to please them, but belonging to the group was more important.

"I tried to convince myself that there must be something wrong with my parents for expecting so much of me. But deep down, I still felt like there was something wrong with me. I needed to continually prove myself to the group. Even then I didn't feel as though I really did fit in and belong."

### EXPLORATION AND DISCOVERY:

Now that you've made a list of what you did to fit in and belong as a teenager, think about how you felt about yourself when you took those actions, then describe your feelings. How many of them are still important to you now?

Teenagers aren't the only ones who need to fit in and belong. For many, this need can extend well beyond the teenage years. You have already discovered that it can continue into adulthood and even into the senior years. In fact, the need for acceptance from others can influence choices that affect an entire lifetime.

The rules for fitting in and belonging as adults may seem less obvious because they appear to be normal, everyday activities for some. It could mean having the ability to out-drink your drinking buddies, or knowing how to order the right vintage wine with dinner. For many, the less obvious way to fit in and belong means having good friends, residing in a nice neighborhood, graduating from a prestigious college or university, having a successful career, membership in a popular country club, going on planned vacations, traveling abroad, having a good amount of wealth, fluently speaking a second language, or something as simple as being liked on Facebook.

### EXPLORATION AND DISCOVERY:

See if you can identify some of the less obvious ways you tried to fit in and belong. Make a list.

The downside of fitting in and belonging is that it doesn't make you feel as good as you thought it would. Why? Because you still never feel quite good enough to really fit in with the group. Even when you accomplish something that should surely impress them, you might end up thinking it wasn't good enough. Introspectively, you think you should have done better. You think you should have purchased a little bigger house or have one-upped everyone with an even better exotic vacation. You think you shouldn't have done it quite that way or said it just like that. For those who are other-dependent, feeling good about a particular accomplishment is so short-lived that it's almost nonexistent. Plus, it is exhausting to continually find ways to impress the group to "fit in." In the end fitting in and belonging doesn't make anyone happy.

The good effects of fitting in and belonging are as temporary as everything else. The high quickly wears off. You are still dependent upon someone or something outside of yourself to feel good and absolutely nothing has changed. And when nothing changes, nothing changes.

> *Life is like a dogsled team…if you're not the lead dog,*
> *the scenery never changes.*
> **—Lewis McDonald Grizzard Jr., American writer and humorist**

As long as you continue to be other-dependent, your need to fit in and belong will not change. Similarly, nothing much can change when you have an exaggerated sense of self-importance and think all eyes are on you. So let's move on to the next chapter where you will learn that you are not the center of everyone else's world.

# It's All About Me

D o you think *they* are talking about you? Well *they* probably aren't. And even if *they* are, so what? Does the idea that *they* might be talking about you bother you?

When we are other-dependent, we think everyone is talking about us because of our exaggerated sense of self-importance. We think all eyes are on us because we believe we are the center of everyone else's life. We even *perform* for everyone around us as though we are on center stage.

## EXPLORATION AND DISCOVERY:

I am sure you remember most of your significant performances. How often have you *performed* for your audience because you thought that all eyes were

continued...

*...continued from previous page*
on you? Who were they for? What was each performance like? Write about them.

We may think everyone is scrutinizing everything about us: how we dress, our weight, the way we style our hair, every wrinkle and zit on our face, and every other "fill-in-the-blank" facet of how we look. We may think they are judging every move we make, everything we say, who we know, what we know and don't know, how much money we appear to have, our lifestyle, our friends, and all the rest of that stuff that bothers you.

### EXPLORATION AND DISCOVERY:

You already have a mental list about the way you think others scrutinize you. Write it down.

You might be surprised to learn that everyone else is thinking the same thing you're thinking. They are thinking all eyes, including yours, are on them. They are thinking you are talking about them. They are thinking you are scrutinizing everything about them. Are you surprised to learn that?

What we have not heretofore known is that most individuals are too busy worrying about how they look to us to pay much attention to how we look. If you find this concept hard to believe, here is an example of how it works.

Have you ever begun telling someone the details about something exciting that has happened to you and before you knew it the other person changed the topic of conversation to themselves and their latest exciting news? Start to pay attention to this phenomenon. It can be a very rude awakening to find out that others don't really pay a whole lot of attention to what happens to you, and if the truth be known, many couldn't care less. This isn't to say that people don't care. It just means that others are not focused on your life in the way you might think they are. It means that each one of us is the center of our own universe, not someone else's.

I realize this doesn't seem to be the case when we watch or listen to the daily news broadcasts that can make it seem as though everyone is paying a lot of attention to everyone else. But carefully notice what happens with today's news headlines. How long do we actually think about what is in the news right this minute before we focus on the next news announcement? How much attention do we really pay to what is happening to someone else even on "breaking news"? A minute or two, if that? Then we get right back to what is far more important to us: what is happening in our own lives and what others might be thinking about it. That should tell you that you are not the focal point of everyone else's attention.

That isn't to say that people don't gossip. But it is to say that when they do gossip it is not because they are interested in you as much as they are interested in looking good to others by knowing the "scoop." In some instances they will even put others down to look better to certain individuals. All of this simply means they are not focused on you the way you might think they are.

Once you actually understand this phenomenon, you will begin to relax.

Thinking that everything is about us often turns into personalizing what others say and do. Personalizing is one of the classic qualities of someone who is other-dependent, and most of the time we don't even realize what we are doing. How do you know if you are personalizing what others say and do? Here's an example of someone personalizing what others say and do.

Let's say you love to walk on the beach. While walking along the water's edge, you pass a couple of guys who are laughing and glancing in your direction. You start to feel self-conscious and are sure they are laughing at you. You are wearing the new bikini you just bought. You begin to worry about how you look. But didn't the sales clerk tell you how fabulous you looked? And you believed her!

Now you are feeling unsure. You have no idea how you really look but are beginning to think that you must look ridiculous. Otherwise, why would these guys be laughing and glancing in your direction? It never occurs to you that someone told a joke, and it was just a fluke that they were looking in your direction. The truth is that they never really noticed you. They were too caught up in their own conversation to pay you any attention. It never computes for you that you are not the center of their world.

This is a perfect example of other-dependency and the lack of self-dependent esteem combined with an exaggerated sense of self-importance. You automatically assume the guys you passed on the beach must be laughing at you because they laughed just as you were walking past them. How could you think otherwise? What else would they be laughing about at the exact same time that you are walking by? You are personalizing because you think everything is about you.

Another example is one that almost everyone on the planet has had at one time or another. You walk into a room full of people and you think everyone is looking at you and judging you. Who hasn't experienced these thoughts when walking into the gym? While you are busy comparing yourself to those with toned, muscular bodies, the real truth is that everyone else is so busy looking at themselves in the mirror that they don't even notice you. You are personalizing because you think all eyes are on you.

When we have no self-dependent esteem, the way we think about ourselves is almost always determined by what we think others think about us. Most of the time we don't even know what they think about us; we just think we know and that's all it takes. We personalize what we think they think and make it our truth. It's as simple as that!

**EXPLORATION AND DISCOVERY:**
What do you think others think about you? Do you personalize what you think others think about you? See if you can remember a time or two when you personalized what you thought someone else was thinking about you. How do you know what they were thinking about you? You made some notes in chapter six to revisit at a later time. They were about identifying what you think others think about you. Let's revisit your notes now. How do they compare to what you think now about what others think about you? Has your thinking about what others think about you changed? If so, in what way has it changed?

When we don't approve of ourselves, we tend to believe someone else's opinion about us regardless of whether it is accurate or not. We might even make up our version of what we think their opinion is about us and believe our own made-up version. In either case, we are personalizing their opinion of us.

**EXPLORATION AND DISCOVERY:**
Do you personalize what others say about you or how they treat you? Do you ever make up your own version of what you think their opinion is about you and believe it?

What people say about you or how they treat you has little to do with you. It is a reflection of how they think about themselves. Their opinion of you is usually based upon their opinion of themselves. Therefore, why bother taking their opinion so personally when it has nothing to do with you? It's all about them and not you.

Besides, when you approve of yourself, you couldn't care less what someone else thinks about you. Very few of us have been taught that it doesn't matter what others think about us. We aren't taught that the only thing that really matters is what *we* think about ourselves.

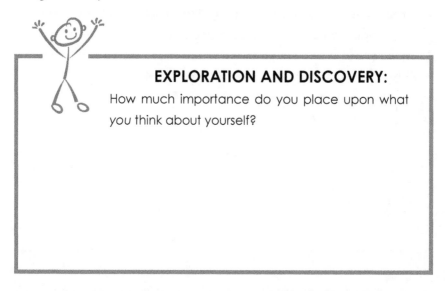

### EXPLORATION AND DISCOVERY:

How much importance do you place upon what you think about yourself?

Terry Cole-Whitaker, writer and author of *What You Think of Me Is None of My Business,* reminds readers in her writings that it doesn't matter what others think about you. She writes, "…if I run my life on the basis of what you think of me, I destroy my own self.…"

What matters most is what you think about you. Since we have already learned that thinking makes it so, let's move on to the next chapter to understand what a difference a thought makes in the way you think about you.

# PART THREE

# Coming Out of My Box

The way out of your box is simple though not always easy in the beginning. You have to make a shift from the negative thoughts and behaviors that have kept you inside the box. You have to replace the unhealthy behaviors you depended upon to make you feel better with a healthy lifestyle that is fun. You have to do something very different from what you are accustomed to doing. You have to celebrate you and positive-up about who you are. You have to repetitively practice thinking positive thoughts about yourself with intention.

# What a Difference a Thought Makes

W e have already established that thought is everything. While life cannot be experienced without it, the type of thoughts we think makes a difference. We create our experience of life with every single thought we think, even though we are not always paying attention to the quality of our thinking. Therefore, life as we experience it is not accidental.

It is estimated that the average person has anywhere from fifty thousand to seventy thousand thoughts daily, and that upwards of 70 to 80 percent of our daily thoughts are negative. Since we are incapable of not thinking (www. ScientificAmerican.com), it logically follows that we need to take charge of the way we think to bring about a desirable experience of life.

The following *Exploration and Discovery* exercise may seem repetitious, but I want to make sure you are able to recognize your thoughts. After all, if you don't know what you're thinking, you can't change it. Monitoring your thinking is the prerequisite for changing your thinking.

**EXPLORATION AND DISCOVERY:**
Notice that you are having thoughts all the time. Those thoughts are not only creating your experience of life, they are creating the way you experience yourself. Especially notice if any of your thoughts are putting you down or making you doubt your ability to create a life experience that includes real happiness from the inside out. Are they saying something like: *This isn't going to work for me* or *I'm not going to be able to do this*? If so, you have to change your thoughts about yourself and what you are capable of achieving. See if you can change them now. What is the outcome?

Who you think you are affects every choice you make and every interaction you have with others. It also affects every feeling you have about yourself and the way you behave in life. Since most of us didn't learn what a difference a thought makes in kindergarten or Life 101, we have to do it now. Who of us grew up knowing that we can make ourselves feel happy anytime we choose to do so? And who knew that it begins with changing a myriad of negative thoughts into a single positive thought that will multiply into more and more positive thoughts? And who would have believed that we could do it all by ourselves with no outside help?

Of course, when we have the ability to think ourselves into being happy, we will no longer be dependent upon the food, alcohol, drugs, antidepressants, money, designer clothes, gambling, job title, or perfect person to make us happy. We will be self-dependent and free to experience real happiness from the inside out. So let's get started.

Oops! Are you thinking that you still don't know how to do this? That is just your negative chatter trying to give you a hard time. It is what your negative chatter has always done while you were paying it no attention. But it's different now. You are paying attention to your negative chatter and you are about to change it.

Even if you are skeptical that this will work, I want you to temporarily suspend your skepticism and do this next *Exploration and Discovery*. I think you will be surprised at what you are capable of doing.

## EXPLORATION AND DISCOVERY:

Think yourself into feeling good. Begin by closing your eyes. Take a deep breath and notice what you are thinking. Just notice whatever it is without making it right or wrong. Then begin thinking about a time when something extra-good happened to you. Think about how good you felt at the time. If you can't think of anything extra-good that has happened to you, you can imagine a "what if" of something extra-good that you would like to experience. Notice how you begin to feel good right now for no particular reason other than that you are thinking about a wonderful time in your life. If and when the negative chatter starts to interfere with your good time, just shift your thoughts back to your good experience. The negative chatter will not give up without a fight. It has been running the show for a long time and is now a habit. So you'll have to remain conscious of your thoughts to shift them to a happy time in your life whenever the negative chatter tries to creep in and ruin your positive thinking experience. Each time you shift from your negative chatter to your good experience is proof that you can do this. Now you know that you can think yourself into feeling good. Now you know what a difference a thought makes.

If for any reason you are unable to think about a happy time in your life, recite a simple nursery rhyme to distract you from your negative chatter until you do think of a happier time.

For example:

Mary had a little lamb
Whose fleece was white as snow.
And everywhere that Mary went,
the lamb was sure to go.
It followed her to school one day
which was against the rule.
It made the children laugh and play,
to see a lamb at school.
And so the teacher turned it out,
but still it lingered near,
And waited patiently about,
till Mary did appear.
"Why does the lamb love Mary so?"
the eager children cry.
"Why, Mary loves the lamb, you know."
the teacher did reply.

Or:

Hey diddle, diddle the Cat and the fiddle,
The Cow jumped over the moon.
The little Dog laughed
To see such sport,
And the dish ran away with the Spoon.

Now think yourself into feeling happy right now for no special reason by simply thinking that you feel happy. Do this by thinking one single happy thought followed by another and another such as:

I feel happy.

I feel happy.

I feel happy now.

I feel happy now for no reason.

I simply feel happy now.

I like feeling happy now.

Feeling happy now is great.

I love feeling happy.

I am responsible for making myself feel happy.

I like being in charge of making myself feel happy right now.

I can feel happy anytime I want to feel happy.

I think I want to feel happy all the time.

I think I can do this.

I think I can make myself feel happy all the time.

### EXPLORATION AND DISCOVERY:

Create your own "thinking yourself into feeling happy right now" mantra. Use it as your new positive message default. Repeat it over and over throughout the day. Notice how happy you feel when you do so. You are experiencing real happiness from the inside out, perhaps for the first time.

Now that you are beginning to experience what a difference a thought really does make and are realizing, perhaps for the first time, that you can change your thoughts from negative to positive, go to www.goodwithme.

com/resources to take an in-depth look at "The Story of You: It's All in Your Head."

In the meantime, let's move on to the next chapter to learn how to celebrate who you are and who you are becoming.

# Celebrate Me!

P eople who have self-dependent esteem celebrate themselves. People who have self-dependent esteem enjoy being who they are. When you are in celebration of yourself, you would rather be you than anyone else in the entire world.

If you have completed the *Exploration and Discovery* assignments up to this point, you have undoubtedly gotten rid of a lot of negative ideas about yourself and are ready to learn how to produce self-dependent esteem. Self-dependent esteem is manufactured by you from within yourself. You are dependent upon yourself for it. You own it! You are no longer other-dependent.

So let's look at the steps that lead to self-dependent esteem. You have already taken the first step by completing the *Exploration and Discovery* assignments. You have gained an insightful understanding about yourself and recognize that being other-dependent and lacking self-dependent esteem has deprived you of real happiness from the inside out.

The next step to self-dependent esteem is usually the most difficult. You actually have to admit that you have none. At first, admitting that you have no self-esteem isn't easy. It can be quite scary. When you have no self-esteem it is almost impossible to admit it. Why? Because the need to look good, the need to be right, and the concern about what other people think of you is still extremely important—right? It's another one of those catch-22s in life. You have to have some measure of self-dependent esteem to admit you don't have self-dependent esteem.

Even harder is admitting that you are dependent upon the approval of others or something else outside yourself for any esteem you do have for yourself. It is usually quite difficult for people who are other-dependent to admit they live for the praise they receive from others. And they certainly don't want to let anyone know they depend upon the opinions of others prior to making decisions. Nor do they want others to know they do whatever it takes to be right in front of others. And heaven forbid they are wrong.

So how do you actually develop self-dependent esteem that allows you to feel good about yourself all the time and in every situation? It's very simple, like growing a garden. You think new healthy thoughts about yourself; the new healthy thoughts take root, then germinate and multiply into more healthy thoughts about yourself until they begin to grow your own special garden variety of self-dependent esteem. It is yours and it is like no other. You don't depend upon anyone else to fertilize it either. You do that yourself by thinking more good thoughts about you.

You have already learned in chapter twenty-six how to silence your negative chatter as well as distract yourself when the negative chatter insists on hanging around, so now all it takes is one single positive thought about yourself. This one positive thought turns into two positive thoughts, which become three positive thoughts, and so forth. It's so simple that anyone can do it, even you. All you have to do is start with one single positive thought about yourself.

**EXPLORATION AND DISCOVERY:**

Think one single positive thought about yourself. I'm sure you can come up with one by now. But if you can't come up with one positive thought about yourself, make one up for now. You could also imagine a "what if" positive thought about yourself that you would like to have, or you can ask a close friend or family member to tell you about a quality they see in you that you don't see in yourself. Or pick one from the list that follows:

- I like the color of my eyes.
- I have healthy legs.
- I have strong toes.
- I am kind.
- I am a good friend.
- I love nature.
- I am a good worker.
- I am a survivor.

Now keep repeating your positive thought over and over throughout the day. What happens? Write about it.

While it is generally the goal of parents and teachers alike to instill self-esteem in every child, many have no idea what actually works. Many educators have a plan for raising test scores but little to no knowledge of how to teach self-esteem. Unfortunately, you cannot teach what you do not know. This is not to say that teachers don't do their best to build self-esteem in children by using whatever tools and programs are made available to them. They definitely deserve credit for their efforts. But if we take a look at the current events in society, it doesn't take much to see that something is sorely missing: the lack of knowledge about self-dependent esteem and other-dependent esteem.

Awareness of the source of your own personal esteem, either from within yourself or from someone or something outside of yourself, provides you with a valuable tool to understand your choices, behaviors, and interactions with others. Fortunately for all of us, taking ownership of our self-esteem is possible. One of my clients, Michael, writes:

I finally accomplished a goal. I have self-esteem now. Looking back, I made starting junior varsity and the backup varsity basketball team, but I quit because I didn't think I was good enough. At age twenty-two I had a walk-on tryout with the St. Louis Cardinals baseball team and didn't try out because I didn't think I was good enough. Today at age fifty I feel great. Life is great. I have accomplished something for the first time in my life and can do it anytime with the confidence I have now and the man I have become who loves life and myself. There's nothing I can't do!

My life has purpose and I don't need mind-altering substances to enjoy it. I used to live in a fog, but life is clearer now. I live in the moment not the past or future. I enjoy life thanks to these classes [at Focus One, which teaches the principles in *Good With Me* in a group setting]. It woke me up! My overall outlook on life is 100 percent better. I love my new life, my freedom. I love the new me. I respect me.

—Michael Clarke

Just because you didn't have self-esteem as a child, or even up until this moment, doesn't mean you can never have it. That is what is so exciting about the science of neuroplasticity, or what the Human Cognition Project calls the "science of our incredible, flexible brain."[15] According to their website, "Neuroplasticity is your brain's ability to create neural pathways and reshape existing ones—even as an adult. Your brain makes these small changes naturally throughout your lifetime. But when neuroplasticity's potential is thoughtfully and methodically explored, this physical reorganization can make your brain faster and more efficient at performing all manner of tasks—no matter how large or small they may be." In other words, "the brain has the innate ability to physically change itself when faced with new, challenging experiences."[16]

This neuro-scientific evidence defies the idea that if you don't have high self-esteem as a child, you can never have it. It defies the well-known cliché that "you can't teach an old dog new tricks." Very simply, this relatively new science establishes that the brain is adaptable. It means you can change your negative chatter to positive thoughts about yourself and that your brain will adjust to these new thoughts. You can change the way you esteem yourself by changing your negative thoughts about yourself to positive ones. As these new positive pathways are strengthened with continued positive thoughts, the positive-thought pathways override the negative-thought pathways. When the negative-thought pathways are no longer being used, they shrink and lose their power. You have created a new default in your brain that is positive!

Anyone can attain self-esteem at any time in life by simply changing the way they think about themselves. How exciting! That is why it is so important that you complete every *Exploration and Discovery* assignment in this book. If you haven't yet done so, please go back and complete them now. Each one is designed to help you change the neural pathways in your brain that are responsible for the way you esteem yourself. You can gain ownership of your self-esteem as an adult and even as a senior adult. It is doable. It is attainable.

Self-development author and speaker Dr. Wayne W. Dyer says, "If you change the way you look at things, the things you look at change." This statement indicates that if you change the way you see yourself, you yourself will change. It's just that simple.

In fact, this process is so simple it sometimes confuses people. We are conditioned to overanalyze almost everything and come up with all types of complicated theories to remedy what seems to be a very complicated life. Being Good With Me isn't complicated. It's really quite simple.

On the other hand, simple doesn't mean easy, as messages like the "Just Say No" anti-drug campaign and Nike's "Just Do It" commercials imply. They make a significant accomplishment sound incredibly easy. While these slogans might make nice sound bites for commercials, the reality is that they are just that: nice, cute slogans that sound clever in advertising jargon. If we could just instantly do whatever we wanted to do, no one would be on drugs, there would be no alcoholics, we would stamp out obesity, and everyone would "be like Mike" (i.e., Michael Jordan).

Because these slogans appear to work in commercials, you might think something is wrong with you when real life isn't that simple and easy—when you just can't say no or just don't do it.

Because simple isn't always easy, especially at first, negative thoughts about yourself will pop up here and there even after you begin thinking the new positive ones. Don't be discouraged. Just notice them. You can even speak to them to distract yourself and to return to your new positive thoughts. And when all else fails, remember you can always recite a nursery rhyme to quickly change your thoughts back to your positive thinking.

**EXPLORATION AND DISCOVERY:**
Speak directly to your negative thoughts when they occur. Have a list ready to combat them before they even happen. Your list can consist of something like this:

Go away.
You don't have a home here anymore.
I'm over you.

*continued...*

*...continued from previous page*

You don't know what you're talking about.

I'm done with you.

You make me laugh.

I don't believe you anymore.

You're toast.

You don't own me anymore.

Now make up some of your own. Write them down to use whenever a negative thought pops into your mind. It's always good to have several methods to overcome negative thoughts.

Good With Me is not a clever slogan that makes a nice advertising sound bite. You have to wake up from your auto-pilot thinking in order to begin living consciously. Keep telling yourself, "Yes, I can do it." You will not only be celebrating yourself, you will begin to "positive-up" about who you are. In fact, let's move on to the next chapter to learn more about how to positive-up.

# Positive-Up!

There isn't anything wrong with you! You don't have character defects! Your personality isn't flawed! Any negative behaviors you thought were just uncontrollable character defects or personality flaws are directly related to your other-dependent esteem and your lack of self-dependent esteem.

**EXPLORATION AND DISCOVERY:**

Make a list of your self-perceived uncontrollable character defects or personality flaws.

Since this list serves no good purpose, it's time to get rid of it.

### EXPLORATION AND DISCOVERY:

Create your own personal ceremony to destroy the list you just made. For example, you can shred it, bury it, or burn it safely in a bowl. Whatever your personal ceremony, be sure it symbolically destroys any residual thinking you may have about your self-perceived character defects and personality flaws.

To positive-up means you no longer allow yourself to think negative thoughts about anyone or anything. This includes you. So now make plans to positive-up about yourself! You have to start depending upon yourself to tell you how great you are even when you don't quite believe it fully.

### EXPLORATION AND DISCOVERY:

Make a list of all the positive qualities about you. Have fun with this. You can even use your imagination and list the qualities you *want* to be true about you. Relish them. Place them on sticky notes everywhere—on your bathroom mirror, on your mobile phone, on the steering wheel of your car, on your desk, in your office cubicle, and any other location where you will see them often. Make sure you look at

*continued...*

*...continued from previous page*
them often. Speak them out loud so that your own ears can hear them. This is the new you!

Whenever you start to revert to your old negative thoughts about yourself, immediately remind yourself to positive-up. You are retraining your brain to think positive thoughts about you.

Bestselling author Deepak Chopra, MD, and Rudolph E. Tanzi, PhD, professor of neurology at Harvard Medical School, champion the power of this kind of thinking in their book *Super Brain*. They write, "You act as leader, inventor, teacher, and user of your brain, all at once." They go on to say,

As leader, you handout the day's orders to your brain.

As inventor, you create new pathways and connections inside your brain that didn't exist yesterday.

As teacher, you train your brain to learn new skills.

As user, you are responsible for keeping your brain in good working order.

They further write, "In these four roles lies the difference between the everyday brain...and what we are calling super brain. Super brain stands for a fully aware creator using the brain to maximum advantage. Your brain is endlessly adaptable." This is further proof that the brain is malleable and capable of being retrained to positive-up—even about yourself!

Practice is important while learning to positive-up. It is also important to remember that practice doesn't make perfect, but instead practice makes better, as we'll learn in the next chapter.

# Practice Makes Better

*To think is to practice brain chemistry.*
—Deepak Chopra, MD

Habits! Habits! Habits! Good habits! Bad habits! Just think about how long and how often you have practiced the habits you currently possess. Whether good or bad, the power of practice has created all of them. You have demonstrated the power of practice with or without your awareness of doing so.

You already know that new habits don't form quickly and easily, but once formed they can be hard to change. You know how much work it takes to break a bad habit. Anything and everything can become a habit, even thinking. If you are one of millions whose thinking has been programmed to default to the negative, you probably don't just think negatively about everyone and everything external to you. You habitually think negatively about yourself as well.

The culprit that denies us total satisfaction in life, otherwise known as happiness, is the *negative way we think about ourselves*. This habit is one of our most practiced and therefore one of the hardest to change. Most of us pay little if any attention to the habitual negative thoughts we have about ourselves. How could something so removed from conscious thought—the way we think about ourselves—have so much power? Years of unconscious practice!

Consider the person who is other-dependent and has a problem with overspending. He probably never gives a second thought to what he is about to do before he goes out and spends money that depletes his bank account, accumulates credit card debt, or both. He likely doesn't recognize that he habitually thinks himself into performing a habitual negative behavior. He probably doesn't hear his negative thoughts that might be saying, *What's wrong with me? Why aren't I more like the guys at the office? They seem to have it all. I feel miserable because I don't like myself right now. So I think I'll go out and spend money I don't have or don't want to spend to buy something nice for myself or to impress the guys at the office. That'll make me feel better.* He probably doesn't realize that this is what he always does to make himself feel better when he feels down or bored or sad or compares himself to others. He is just one of many that actor Will Smith was referring to when he said, "Too many people spend money they haven't earned, to buy things they don't want, to impress people they don't like." Likewise, this man probably won't pay much attention to the barrage of negative thoughts about himself after the adrenalin rush of spending money is over. They are thoughts like *I hate it when I do this. I feel so guilty. What's wrong with me? Why can't I stop? I am so dumb.*

Subsequently, he is filled with regret about his actions when he doesn't have enough money left in his bank account to make his mortgage payment. He gets mad at himself and even calls himself names like stupid and idiot among others. But this isn't the end of the situation he created for himself. He feels miserable all over again when the credit card statements come in. Once again he criticizes himself for being such a stupid idiot. In his situation, thinking about spending money irresponsibly after the fact doesn't prevent the behavior, nor does it change the negative thoughts he has about himself. It has become a habitual response to feeling bad, and he does it automatically with no thought about its repercussions. Once done, he puts himself down, feels even worse about himself, and repeats this cycle over and over in his attempt to feel better. Long practice has made his negative habit so powerful that it will be hard to break.

**EXPLORATION AND DISCOVERY:**

Can you think of any negative behaviors you've engaged in over and over just to make yourself feel better? Make a list. Can you recognize any of the repetitive negative thoughts you have had about yourself as a result of your habitual negative behaviors? Make a list. Did it ever occur to you that you are very good at resorting to these negative behaviors and thoughts because practice makes better?

Most of the harmful automatic, even addictive, behaviors we have already addressed became habits without our awareness, even the habit of calling ourselves stupid. As a result, you like many others have muddled through life trying to make yourself feel as good as possible, in any way you can, without a clue that there is a better way.

Here is your clue to a better way. Practice makes whatever you practice better. Some of you are already making significant positive changes that will become habitual with practice. Some of you are not. What's up with that? Why will some of you keep looking for the next best self-help book, conference, or event to get the help you need? What is the difference between the person who makes positive life changes and the person who doesn't? Some people read a book or go to a workshop, practice nothing, and just sort of think about it, while others become very good at practicing positive habits. As an example, Tiger Woods is very good at practicing golf. Michael

Jordan was very good at practicing basketball. What do you want to be good at practicing?

Practice may sound like drudgery. More work than fun. Whatever it is for you will depend upon the way you think about it. Will you think it is work, or will you think yourself into having fun with it?

## EXPLORATION AND DISCOVERY:

Practice esteeming who you are. Make a list of words that are self-esteeming. These words begin with "self."

- Self-prideful
- Self-admiring
- Self-approving
- Self-confident
- Self-important
- Self-loving
- Self-respecting
- Self-satisfied

Add your own self-esteeming words to this list. Notice that these words are about you esteeming yourself and have nothing to do with the way others esteem you. They have nothing to do with approval from others, looking good to others, being right, or controlling the way others think about you. They have nothing to do with your material possessions, education, knowledge, accomplishments, friends, or money in the bank. They exist within you just because you exist and not because of what you have, do, or know. They are an expression of you just because you are you. Be sure to make the practice of esteeming yourself a fun experience.

*continued...*

*...continued from previous page*

Utilize the positive thinking-feeling-doing loop as you practice esteeming yourself. The loop works like this. You think a self-esteeming word about yourself, which leads to feeling esteem for who you are. When you feel esteem for who you are your behavior will reflect the esteem you have for you. For example, the more you esteem who you are the easier it is for you to see yourself with softer and kinder eyes; you begin to see past what you have, do, and know. Your reaction to this will be holding your head high with self-pride no matter what. This prompts another self-esteeming word that engenders feelings of contentment, satisfaction, and happiness. These feelings foster kindness toward you. Your kindness toward yourself provokes more acceptance of yourself, which you act out in your everyday routine, and the loop continues without end. This is the powerful self-esteeming thinking-feeling-doing loop at work.

The goal of practice is that practice makes better™. You could become very good at practicing until the self-esteeming positive thoughts about you are all that remain. You may become so good at practicing that you don't even remember how you once lacked self-dependent esteem. How great is that? It is great but only if you are not expecting the results of your practice to be perfect. You set yourself up to fail when perfection is the goal—it's too easy to give up when you fall short of the mark.

Practice is almost never perfect. Practice is working toward getting better. You complicate your practice sessions with the idea that your practice has to be perfect. Practice doesn't have to be perfect because it is *practice*. Practice is working to improve a skill. If you were already perfect, you couldn't get any better. So why bother to practice?

Even though practice always makes better and not perfect, greater results are possible when you practice with deliberate intention. The next chapter shows you how to achieve greater results through practice with deliberate intention.

## CHAPTER THIRTY

# Deliberate Intentional Practice Makes Better Faster

I n the arenas of elite performers and athletes, a concept called "intentional" or "deliberate" practice has been closely studied. While practice is a powerful tool for these individuals, practice that is deliberate and intentional increases the power of practice exponentially and desired results occur more rapidly. It's all about getting what you want with greater speed and maximum efficiency.

Remember, do not confuse the concept of deliberate intentional practice with the adage "practice makes perfect." Perfection is not the point here. The point is that practice makes better, and deliberate intentional practice makes us better faster. Even Michael Jordan made mistakes in his amazing basketball career. Those mistakes never prevented him from practicing again and again. And in the end, because he practiced with deliberate intention, his mistakes actually made him better—not perfect, but better faster.

The concept of deliberate intentional practice has been around for some time, so let's take a look at what has been discovered about it.

Geoffrey Colvin, author of *Talent Is Overrated: What Really Separates World-Class Performers from Everybody Else* and a senior editor-at-large for *Fortune* magazine, writes about the extensive research that helped to disprove the theory that elite performers and athletes are simply born with innate talent.

For example, Tiger Woods wasn't genetically born a great golfer. He had to work to become a masterful golfer. Just like the rest of us who have to practice to be good at something, he too has to practice to be good at his game. Since many of us have practiced a skill at some time or another, is there a difference between the way we practice and the way Tiger Woods practices? The research of K. Anders Ericsson, Ralf Th. Krampe, and Clemens Tesch-Romer, who published "The Role of Deliberate Practice in the Acquisition of Expert Performance," suggests that there is a difference. They write, "…individuals begin in their childhood a regimen of effortful activities (deliberate practice) designed to optimize improvement." In order to become a masterful golfer, Tiger learned to practice with deliberate intention as a toddler. Similarly, Mozart was a three-year-old when he began playing the piano.

So just what is practice with deliberate intention? According to Colvin's theory, it is hours of focused repetitive daily practice on a specific goal, paying close attention to what works and what doesn't, and correcting what doesn't work.

As you can see, there is a difference between deliberate intentional practice and just plain practice. Deliberate intentional practice requires focus and conscious awareness. Deliberate intentional practice requires that you focus on a desired outcome. It requires that you focus on practice techniques and visualize the desired outcome in your mind's eye. It includes paying attention to what works as well as what doesn't work and taking corrective action accordingly.

For those who are other-dependent, deliberate intentional practice requires awareness of your need to look good and be right. It requires that you give yourself permission not to be immediately good at everything and not to know everything about everything all the time. It is becoming comfortable with imperfection.

Deliberate intentional practice will shift your other-dependent esteem to self-dependent esteem at a more rapid pace. It requires the same kind of focus and conscious awareness that is required for any skill you want to improve. To make the shift from other-dependent esteem to self-dependent esteem you have to visualize the end result: feeling good about you without depending upon anyone or anything outside of yourself to make you happy. You have to focus for hours daily on this goal and pay close attention to the results of your practice, taking corrective action whenever you fall short of your goal.

So what does that mean? It means you have to pay close enough attention to your thoughts so that you will notice a shift from self-esteeming positive thoughts back to the negative ones when it occurs, and take corrective action to shift the negative thoughts to self-esteeming ones.

To shift your other-dependent esteem to self-dependent esteem, you have to believe your self-esteeming positive thoughts about yourself. Up until now the Exploration and Discovery assignments have included monitoring your thoughts to become aware of what kind of thoughts you are thinking to enable you to practice changing your negative thoughts to positive thoughts. Once you could begin changing your negative thoughts to positive thoughts, you could begin to use the thinking-feeling-doing loop to practice esteeming yourself. Now it is time for you to believe that you have worth and value just because you exist.

### EXPLORATION AND DISCOVERY:

Practice believing the self-esteeming positive thoughts about yourself with deliberate intention. Focus on your specific goal of esteeming you without depending upon anyone or anything outside of you to give you approval or make you look good. Monitor the way you feel about yourself

*continued...*

*...continued from previous page*
to know if you are beginning to believe the self-esteeming positive thoughts you are having about yourself. Do you notice a shift in the way you feel? Are you beginning to believe the self-esteeming positive thoughts you are having about you? Are you internalizing them? Are you taking ownership of them and making them yours for real? Take corrective action to shift from uncertainty to belief. Counter every negative thought with a self-esteeming positive thought.

Use your practice list of self-esteeming positive thoughts from chapter 29 to support your corrective action and deepen your belief that you have real value from the inside out.

Begin by paying attention to the thoughts that truly help you esteem yourself from the inside out just because you exist.

- Which ones are easier to believe?
- Which self-esteeming thoughts work best to make you feel good/happy?
- Notice the thoughts that don't work and eliminate them.
- Repeat the thoughts that make you believe you have value just because you exist over and over with deliberate intention.
- Create a self-esteeming mantra about you by using the thoughts that invoke self-esteem.
- Practice reciting your self-esteeming mantra hour after hour throughout the day with deliberate intention.

Next, pay attention to your thinking patterns.

- Are there times when self-esteeming thoughts are more prevalent?
- Are certain self-esteeming thoughts easier to notice than others?

*continued...*

*...continued from previous page*

- Are there times when you resist the idea of thinking something good about yourself?
- Are there times when the need for approval from others is more prevalent?
- Are certain needs for approval from others easier to catch than others?

Now, pay attention to what works and what doesn't work to negate the need for approval from others.

- What works best to turn your self-critical putdowns into positive feedback?
- Do you notice a power struggle between your need for approval from others and your self-esteeming thinking?
- What prohibits you from thinking self-esteeming thoughts about yourself?
- What fosters self-esteeming thoughts?
- Give yourself honest and direct feedback about what does and doesn't work.
- Improve upon what worked with deliberate intentional practice.

As you practice with deliberate intention, you will shift your other-dependent esteem to self-dependent esteem in no time. It will occur faster than you might have imagined possible.

Of course, you and I both know what happens when you get to the end of a book without taking time to practice the desired goals—nothing much! You have gained some new left-brain information and that's about it; nothing will change without practice. Now you not only know that practice makes better, you know that practicing with deliberate intention makes better happen faster.

**EXPLORATION AND DISCOVERY:**
Make a list of what you are consciously doing to shift your other-dependent esteem to self-dependent esteem. Make a list of what you are changing to eliminate the need for someone or something outside of yourself to make you happy. Make a list of the various ways you are now able to make yourself happy all by yourself.

Without a doubt, your other-dependent esteem has already begun to shift to self-dependent esteem. Keep your eye on your desired goal and make all of your deliberate intentional practice repetitive as you go forward. The following chapter will outline the benefits of repetition.

# Repetition Works

The sports greats practice with repetitive deliberate intention. They don't just practice once in a while and expect to win. Nor do they call it a day after putting the ball through the hoop a few times.

Great athletes and performers recognize that repetition works. If you doubt that even a little bit just look at how well it worked in making you other-dependent. Current research corroborates the concept of repetition by suggesting that 98 percent of the thoughts you have today are the same thoughts you had the day before. If you even slightly question the idea that repetition works, just think about how well your repetitive negative thoughts have worked up till now. How much more proof do you need that repetition works?

Every publicist and advertising agency knows that a good advertising campaign must be repetitive to achieve a specific goal. Likewise, you not only have to practice thinking good thoughts about yourself with deliberate intention, you have to repetitively do so day after day. You have to think those good thoughts over and over and over and over and over again to achieve the results you desire. It may feel odd or uncomfortable at first, but do it anyway. Soon it will feel as natural as breathing.

You are going to have to delete all uncomplimentary thoughts about yourself from your repertoire and replace them with new self-esteeming positive thoughts. In order to do so, it is time for you to start your own personal Good With Me advertising campaign.

## EXPLORATION AND DISCOVERY:

Begin your own personal Good With Me advertising campaign by showering yourself with praise over and over for hours every day. Make a list, a very long list, of complimentary words to repeat to yourself about yourself. Choose at least one complimentary word to repeat each day. Repeat it all day long. Notice how you feel at the end of the day.

Here are some examples of complimentary messages to repeat for hours every day. Notice that these complimentary messages have nothing to do with what you have, do, or know. They are complimentary of you just because you are you and you exist.

- I like me.
- I like who I am.
- I know that who I am is good enough.
- I have a good opinion of myself.
- I approve of myself.

- I am valuable and worthy.
- I respect me.
- I trust me.
- I am free to be me.
- I love me!
- I'm totally good with me!

Add some of your own messages to your list, remembering they are not about what you have, do, or know. Repeat these phrases with deliberate intention every day. Do it even if you don't believe them at first. Do it anyway and you'll be amazed at the results. Repetition works, and it won't be long before you begin to own them. The way you feel about yourself will start to change. When it does, you will want to have a way to measure the results of your practice, so continue on to the next chapter to learn how to measure your success.

## CHAPTER THIRTY-TWO

# The Measures of Success

I n athletics, the players can look at statistics, scores, and games won to help them gauge how they're doing. They have coaches and trainers standing by to give them feedback and direction in their quest to become skillful in their chosen sport.

Unlike athletes, your measures of success aren't going to be available to you in numbers and percentages. While there's no scoreboard tracking your success, there are visible indicators that tell you that your repetitive deliberate intentional practice is moving you in the right direction.

Awareness of the internal conversation you are having with yourself— also known as your internal chatter or self-talk—and the role it plays in what you do and how you feel is significant. Most people have a little voice chattering away in their heads all day long. It's detrimental to growing self-dependent esteem when no one is paying any attention to its negative criticisms. That's when the negative thoughts have full rein over us—when no one is charting the negative chatter. You are moving in the right direction when you can begin to hear your negative chatter and recognize that you're the initiator of it.

A noticeable sign that you are gaining some self-dependent esteem is that the ongoing negative chatter will no longer exist in the forefront of your mind. The negative chatter may not totally disappear at first, but you will notice that it's moving further and further to the back of your thoughts.

The Four Attachments we discussed in chapters five through nine—(1) the need for approval from others, (2) the need to look good, (3) the need to be right, and (4) the need to control outcomes—will fade away along with the negative voice in your head. You will notice that what other people are thinking about you doesn't matter so much. You'll no longer allow others to victimize you with the way they think about you, nor will you continue to victimize yourself with your own thoughts.

Another noticeable measure of success is when your internal conversations begin to change. Instead of saying *Why are those people laughing at me? They must be laughing at me because I look weird,* the little voice that used to put you down has changed to *Look at those people laughing. They must be having fun.* In other words, you start to realize that not everything is about you. With that realization, your level of self-consciousness will lessen. You'll stop personalizing everything. Your exaggerated sense of self-importance will begin to disappear. You'll become more aware of the existence of other people, and you will be more aware of your surroundings.

Your measure of success will also be evidenced by the way you feel. As you engage in deliberate intentional practice to change your thoughts and actualize self-dependent esteem, you will have to listen closely to your own internal barometer to measure your success. Your internal barometer in this case is the way you feel. You'll discover that little signals will start appearing that tell you that you are making the switch from other-dependent esteem to self-dependent esteem. For example, you suddenly feel happy out of the blue. You unexpectedly feel good about yourself for no particular reason. Consider this as feedback with which to gauge your success. You begin to see yourself through softer and kinder eyes. Much to your surprise, you appreciate who you are. Consider this as an indicator of your success. Without rhyme or reason, you like yourself just because you are you. To your amazement and without warning, you all of a sudden feel happiness from the inside out. This is an indication that you are succeeding at being Good With Me.

**EXPLORATION AND DISCOVERY:**
Chart your success by paying attention to how good/happy you feel. Notice how much better you feel about yourself with no strings attached.

You still might be wondering, *Who's going to be my coach? Who's going to motivate me?* Well, guess what? You will be your own coach because believe it or not you're the best person for the job. You will motivate you from the inside out because all motivation comes from within oneself. You will motivate yourself to go to www.goodwithme.com/resources for support. When it comes to changing your thinking, acquiring self-dependent esteem, or experiencing real happiness from the inside out, all motivation is self-motivation, no matter what the motivational coaches of the world would have you believe. A motivational coach can rah-rah you to the max, but it is you who has to make a decision to do something about what they present to you. You have to motivate yourself with the way you think. This is not to say that motivational coaches aren't important. They provide valuable information, guidance, and support, but it is you who must motivate yourself to implement their teachings. Clearly, you know yourself best and only you know that crucial moment when you are ready for change. You will put forth the required effort to become Good With Me when you motivate yourself to do so.

Despite any skepticism to the contrary, you are already at the crucial moment. You are already self-motivated. You would not have opened this book if you hadn't been. And you surely would not have continued to this page for the sheer fun of it. However, you can continue going forward from here for the pure fun of it!

## EXPLORATION AND DISCOVERY:

Notice how much fun it is to keep track of the increase in your positive internal chatter. Notice how much fun it is to measure your success as a positive thinker.

While you are having fun measuring your success as a positive thinker, it is important to be mindful of the words you think and speak. Some seemingly innocent words can thwart your success with their negative effects and you might not even know it. So let's take a look at the power of these words in the next chapter.

# Word Power

The words we speak have power. Certain words have more power than others. There are positive replacement words for some of them and there are a few words to avoid altogether because of their negative implication. The words we are going to look at closely are *try, can't, but, wish, hope,* and *problem.*

**EXPLORATION AND DISCOVERY:**
Pay attention to your use of the words *try, can't, but, wish, hope,* and *problem.* For now, make a mental note whenever you think or speak them.

The word *try* is often an avoidance word. It is also a word to avoid using when you really want to say no. It is most often used to avoid doing an unpleasant or difficult task that you have been asked to do. For example: A close friend asks you to help him move on Saturday morning at the same time you had planned to play golf. You don't want to give up your plans, and you don't want to disappoint your friend by saying no to his request. And above all you don't want to risk losing his approval. So your response to your friend might be "I'll *try* to be there," which probably means "I don't want to tell you that I won't be there." Because you are other-dependent and worry about what your friend will think of you for saying no, you avoid telling him you won't be there. You don't want him to be mad at you either. So instead of just saying no, you don't show up and then you make up some kind of excuse that allows you to save face.

### EXPLORATION AND DISCOVERY:

Recall a time when you used the word *try* to avoid doing something you didn't want to do because it allowed you to save face at a later time. Can you recall how you felt?

The word *try* almost always leaves you with a way out and almost always means no. So why not just say no? Because you are other-dependent and afraid of what others will think about you when you do. In this example, the golfer's self-esteem takes a hit because he isn't honest with his friend. But you probably know that it's difficult to be honest when you're worried about what others think of you. It's especially difficult when you want everyone to like you and approve of you.

Even Yoda in *The Empire Strikes Back* has something to say about the word *try*. He says, "Try? There is no try; only do or do not."

To illustrate what Yoda meant, let's *try* the following experiment.

Place an object on the table in front of you. *Try* to pick it up. Were you successful in picking it up? If so, then you didn't *try*. If you actually picked it up, you *did* it. You cannot pick up the object when you are *trying*. *Trying* does nothing. You either pick it up or you don't. Go ahead and *try* again. Nothing happens when you *try* to pick it up. If the object remains on the table, you *tried* to pick it up. But since *try* doesn't do anything the object remains on the table; you simply can't pick it up when all you do is *try* to pick it up.

While *try* gives you wiggle room, it is different from saying no with justification. Saying no instead of *I'll try* is an honest expression. Honest expression is often difficult for those who are other-dependent. We haven't been taught that it is all right to just say no. And by the way, the word no is often a complete sentence. It is okay to say no without justification even when others are waiting with bated breath for an explanation that justifies our saying no.

**EXPLORATION AND DISCOVERY:**
Use repetitive deliberate intentional practice to say no instead of *I'll try* when a situation calls for doing so. Are you able to stop yourself from saying *I'll try*? Can you say no without justification? Do you still have the need to justify saying no? Do you feel different about yourself when you say no? Write about your results.

Similarly, *can't* is another word to be mindful of when you're doing a negative chatter evaluation of yourself. Why? The word *can't* is disempowering because it almost always translates to the word *won't*. *Can't* is another cop-out word that is often used as an excuse to avoid saying no. In the previous example of the friend asking you to help him move, you might respond with "I *can't* because I'm playing golf," instead of the more truthful response, "I *won't* be there because I have plans to play golf that morning."

In this situation, *can't* is an avoidance word that indicates helplessness. It seems to say there's nothing you can do to change your golf plans, whereas *won't* signifies that you are not helpless and are making a choice. The reality is that you can help your friend if you choose to help him. But you are choosing not to help him and to play golf as planned. The word *can't* reduces the risk of your friend's disapproval. In this example, as in the example of the word *try*, being direct and honest with your friend would be a sign of self-dependent esteem.

### EXPLORATION AND DISCOVERY:
Use deliberate intentional practice to avoid using the word *can't* in your speaking. Notice what you feel when you do so, and write about it.

There are two more avoidance words that in certain contexts can keep you stuck inside of your box. They are *wish* and *hope*. For example, "*Wishing* you would win the lottery so that you won't be stressed out about money all the time." Or "*Hoping* things change for the better pretty soon." These two words when spoken in this context change nothing. You are quite likely to keep on *wishing* and *hoping* without taking any real action to address the situation. These are avoidance words because they give us an excuse to avoid taking action to make the changes we are *wishing* and *hoping* for.

## EXPLORATION AND DISCOVERY:

Pay attention to your *wishing* and *hoping* thoughts. Can you see how they are keeping you stuck not only inside of your box, but in your life? Notice how often you utilize these two words.

The word *but* is another avoidance word. It is a word that negates everything that precedes it. For example, if you tell a friend she looks good today, but you think she looks better in pink, what did you actually just tell her? You certainly didn't tell her that she looks good today because the word *but* negated the words that preceded it.

If you want to tell a friend she looks good today without negating your compliment while saying you think she looks better in pink, replace the word *but* with *and*. So here's what your compliment would look like: "You look good today, *and* I think you look even better in pink." Use of the word *and* changes the context of your compliment. In this example, she still looks good and she looks even better in pink. Can you hear the difference?

**EXPLORATION AND DISCOVERY:**

Use repetitive deliberate intentional practice to replace the word *but* with the word *and*. What do you notice?

Now let's address the final word on my list of words to avoid when making positive changes: the word *problem*. There is so much to say about this word that I want you to go to www.goodwithme.com/resources for a free article titled "Problem vs. Stuff." I'll give you a preview though. Whenever we label something as a *problem* we think differently about it. We may even stress about the *problem*. *Stuff*, to the contrary, is just *stuff*. It is easy to handle. No stressing over *stuff* because we have a different view of *stuff*.

**EXPLORATION AND DISCOVERY:**

Use repetitive deliberate intentional practice to replace the word *problem* with *stuff*. Notice what happens. And be sure to check out the entire article "Problem vs. Stuff" on www.goodwithme.com/resources.

In the meantime, prepare to come out of your box by putting you first and others second. Sound impossible? Well, go on to the next chapter to learn how to put yourself first and others second and take the scariness out of putting yourself first as well.

# PART FOUR

# I'm Out of My Box!

You practice healthy selfishness when you are out of your box. It's you first and others second. You give yourself permission to play, to have real fun, and to do nothing at all. You stop resisting life and enjoy acceptance of yourself and others. You use the positive thinking loop. You see the good and positive in yourself and others. You reinvent yourself. You are self-dependent and experience real happiness from the inside out. And above all else you are Good With Me!

# Me First, You Second

"Me first, you second" is an attitude that few of us were conditioned to believe is okay. Putting ourselves first is frowned upon by many. While taking care of "me first, you second" is completely opposite of what most of us have been taught, there's more to the concept than you might think.

First of all, many of us put others first because we want them to like us and have a good opinion of us. Others do it because we have been conditioned to think it's the only right thing to do. Like me, you may have been taught that you are a better person when you take care of everyone else before yourself. We are considered virtuous if we take care of everyone else prior to tending to our own needs. Many of us notice that people like us better when we are selfless.

There's a general misconception in our society that selfishness is bad and that it's wrong to put yourself before others. Selfishness has a negative connotation. The phrases "it's all about me" and "looking out for number one" imply that you are conceited, arrogant, or self-centered.

They very seldom imply that you are a healthy individual who has self-dependent esteem.

Another one of my clients, Temple, says, "I live for me. I take care of me first." We have a right to take good care of ourselves. It is important to give ourselves permission to be selfish. We have to be selfish in order to have selfness. Jacquelyn Small, author of *Transformers*, writes, "Selfishness is a stepping stone to Self-ness. We cannot give to someone else something we do not ourselves possess. So we must develop a Self in order to give this Self to others." She emphasizes the idea that selfishness is healthy. To practice *healthy selfishness* you have to give yourself permission to put yourself first and others second.

If you have ever traveled by air, you have witnessed the flight attendant announcement that instructs you to put on your own oxygen mask first. You are given permission to put you first and others second.

## EXPLORATION AND DISCOVERY:
Give yourself permission to put you first and others second. Notice how you think and feel when you first begin to practice healthy selfishness with deliberate intention.

Healthy selfishness serves a purpose. It equips us to carry on, thrive, and be available to others. Healthy selfishness can feel very uncomfortable for the person conditioned by society to take care of everyone else first. You might even feel guilty at first. Push through the guilt. Don't let it stop you.

Unhealthy selfishness serves a purpose as well, but there is a distinction between healthy selfishness and unhealthy selfishness. While unhealthy selfishness equips us to carry on and thrive, we put ourselves first at the expense of others and are available to no one. For example, those who exhibit traits of unhealthy selfishness may put themselves first and others second by lying to get approval, cheating to get ahead, backstabbing to be liked, arguing to be right, and using a myriad of substances to make them unavailable to others.

Being selfish enough to take good care of you first is equivalent to giving yourself the gift that keeps on giving. To the contrary, people who give to others first often end up being empty and used up with nothing left to give to anyone, even to themselves.

Recount how much time you have left over to take care of yourself when you are busy putting everyone else first. If not much, you are probably feeling resentment toward others. When you sacrifice yourself for others while not taking care of yourself first, you end up resenting those you are helping. And it really isn't their fault. They have a right to ask you for what they want from you; you can't control that. Even though they might expect you to put them first because that is what you have always done, you are the one making the choice to do so. It is up to you to say no when helping them is hurting you.

### EXPLORATION AND DISCOVERY:

Think about the times when you have resented someone you were helping. Have you ever wondered when it would be your turn to be taken care of? Have you thought or said "After all I've done for you...?" If so, make a list of those times.

Learning how to say no when saying yes does not take care of you is actually learning how to set healthy boundaries to protect yourself. Contrary to what you might be thinking right now, setting healthy boundaries and practicing healthy selfishness does not mean you stop caring for others. When you make yourself a priority and establish healthy boundaries, you end up with more to give to others. It's like taking care of yourself first so you can care for your child. This is a win-win situation for everyone.

Go to www.goodwithme.com/resources for a free article titled "Don't Give All Your Water Away."

Besides, you can't keep putting yourself last and still think you are as important as everyone else. The two don't go together. How can you ever feel good about yourself when you are always last in line? Whatever happened to taking turns? It's a good concept, but sometimes we literally have to *take* our turn when others won't offer it. We have to stand up for ourselves. Saying no to others can have an enormous positive effect upon your overall satisfaction in life because you are taking responsibility for taking good care of yourself.

People who don't take good care of themselves are often very angry and act out their anger in a myriad of ways. Their anger could explode and manifest itself as physical bullying, verbal abuse, domestic violence, and even murder. Conversely, it could implode and manifest as self-criticism, self-loathing, self-mutilation, and even suicide.

Numerous studies show that anger management seldom works, but some of you already know that. The key to dissipating anger is self-dependent esteem. With that, the anger disappears. It's almost like magic. How can we not be angry when we think we're not good enough or when there seems to be something wrong with us?

When you take care of everyone else first, you give yourself the message that you aren't as important as they are. When you take care of yourself first, you actually give your own psyche the message that you are just as important as everyone else. You give yourself the message that you have as much value as they have, that you are just as worthy. This is the beginning of making a shift to the positive thinking-feeling-doing loop for you.

You can make the switch from other-dependent esteem to self-dependent esteem by doing all of the things for yourself that you have been doing for others. You stop waiting around for others to reciprocate your good deeds. Instead, you nurture yourself.

**EXPLORATION AND DISCOVERY:**

Nurture yourself. Do all the things for yourself that you do for others. Do the things for yourself that you want others to do for you.

As you nurture yourself your own psyche will notice the change. It could feel uncomfortable at first but don't quit. Keep on nurturing yourself and before you know it you will think that you have value. When you treat yourself as though you count you will begin to have a healthy sense of self-importance. The more times you repetitively practice nurturing yourself with deliberate intention, the quicker your thinking about yourself will change—and the sooner it will be comfortable to put you first and others second.

You might find this hard to believe, but it's a compliment when the people you have always placed before yourself accuse you of becoming selfish. They have just provided you with evidence that your practice is working. You are moving in a healthy and positive direction.

## EXPLORATION AND DISCOVERY:

When someone tells you how selfish you are becoming as you practice healthy selfishness by setting boundaries, respond with a simple "thank you." They don't realize they have actually given you a compliment. Their compliment is proof that your repetitive practice with deliberate intention is working for you. You no longer have to take care of everyone else first so that they like you and have a good opinion of you. Pleasing others is no longer your first priority. You are shifting from other-dependent esteem to self-dependent esteem.

When you change the source of your esteem from other-dependent to self-dependent, you are in control of the one and only thing you can control: you. You alone determine the direction your life journey takes. And now that you are out of your box, oh what fun it can be. So let's move on to the next chapter to make sure you know how to have fun and plenty of it.

# What Fun It Is!

A re you having fun yet? Real fun is out of reach for those who are other-dependent. Even the illusion of fun isn't much fun. But the good news is that your definition of fun changes when you become self-dependent. Your thinking changes too and you begin to have fun in ways you never before thought possible.

Most of us haven't been taught how to have fun beyond the experience of childhood, and we've forgotten how good it feels to have fun for real. Those who are other-dependent are afraid to look silly, so for many the only time they can "let their hair down" and play is when they're intoxicated or high. Otherwise it is too uncomfortable to play.

To the contrary, self-dependent people give themselves permission to play. They have lightened up because they no longer depend upon what others think of them.

**EXPLORATION AND DISCOVERY:**
What kind of child's play would you like to indulge in now that you are no longer afraid you might look foolish to others? Write a short description.

There are as many reasons not to have fun as there are ways to have fun. Let's explore a few of the reasons why we won't give ourselves permission to play. Some of us have been taught to take life seriously, so there's no time for play. Some of us have been conditioned to believe it's irresponsible to be "clowning around like a child." Some may even think they're not very good at child's play. To that end, ask yourself how you could not be good enough just to play and have some fun. You might remember how self-conscious you were when you were playing as a child, and that memory keeps you from playing now. Could it be that even as a child you were worried about what others thought of you, even while playing?

Others think they are too old to do something just for the fun of it. Don't wait until retirement to have fun. Don't put it off. It's time to have some real fun now. Having fun doesn't wait until someday when you're ready.

Those who are self-dependent don't have to depend upon a distraction from life to have fun. People who feel good about themselves have fun all day long, every day. They make everything they do fun. They simply think themselves into having fun and feeling good even when not engaged in playful activities.

Remember that even when learning how to have fun, practice is just practice. You're not striving for perfection, you're just having fun. Of course, repetitive deliberate intentional practice makes everything you do become fun even faster.

**EXPLORATION AND DISCOVERY:**
Practice having fun with deliberate intention. Make having fun an adventure. Use your imagination and go on your fun adventure. Write about the results.

Sadly, most of us have been taught to take life far too seriously. In the grand scheme of things it doesn't really matter if we go through life playing the whole time or not. Our lifetime goes by either way. No one really cares whether we have fun or not. It's up to us. Remember, it's never too late to have fun like a child again.

**EXPLORATION AND DISCOVERY:**
Find out how it feels to have fun like a child. Make a list of ways to play. Make a list of anything and everything you think could be fun for you. Then choose one thing from your list and do it within the week. Chart your level of fun.

Even the smallest activity is fun for those who are self-dependent because they are naturally "high on life." What does this mean? It means they think themselves into feeling good naturally without a dependency of any kind. They think themselves into feeling good for no apparent reason other than "just because." It's all in the thinking!

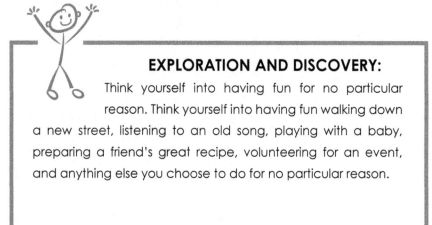

**EXPLORATION AND DISCOVERY:**
Think yourself into having fun for no particular reason. Think yourself into having fun walking down a new street, listening to an old song, playing with a baby, preparing a friend's great recipe, volunteering for an event, and anything else you choose to do for no particular reason.

Everything in life is a lot more fun when you stop resisting it. With that in mind, let's go to the next chapter to understand what can happen when you accept that everything just is what it is.

# It Is What It Is

T he acceptance of "it is what it is" is the exact opposite of the need to control the outcome of everything. In modern jargon "it is what it is" means that we accept things for the way they really are.

Acceptance of this concept puts an end to your resistance to life. It puts an end to the struggle and the bad times. Even self-dependent individuals may not always like every circumstance that occurs, but they know and accept that it is what it is. For example, we may not always like the way we said something, but we said it the way we said it. Acceptance that it is what it is gives us inner happiness. Very simply, happiness is the acceptance of what is.

Since everything is just what it is, why not accept it? This is not to suggest that acceptance means liking or even condoning our circumstances. It simply means accepting things the way they are so that we can do something about changing them if we desire to do so.

**EXPLORATION AND DISCOVERY:**
Practice accepting that it is what it is. How do you feel when you do? If you truly accept that "whatever" is what it is, you will notice that any stress you were experiencing begins to diminish. Your whole body will start to relax.

What you resist persists. Most of us don't understand that what we resist not only persists, it gets bigger. In other words the more you resist "it is what it is," the more it persists and the larger it becomes. This concept has to do with the universal law of attraction. You actually attract more of what you are resisting because it becomes your dominant thought. Remember, thinking makes it so!

Psychology suggests we always move in the direction of our dominant thought and create more of it for ourselves, whether negative or positive. That's great if you are moving toward what you want, and not so great if you are moving toward something you are resisting. For example, if you fear the loss of your relationship partner, you will behave in a way that pushes her away. You might become very needy, insecure, jealous, and even spiteful. As a result of your unattractive behavior, you will make what you fear happen. You will push her away. Resistance actually slows down or mitigates your progress in getting what you really want.

Acceptance of "it is what it is" puts an end to our resistance of the way things really are. How do you accept something or someone you greatly dislike? How exactly do you accept something you despise without giving in to it or giving up your convictions?

Quite simply, you accept that which you can't change or control. You can't make it be something it isn't. All you can do is accept it for what it is, move away from it, and move on with your life. That is not to say you can't crusade for your beliefs. You just have to know that nothing or no one changes because of you. You can't change people. People make changes because it is what they really want for themselves.

Yes, we live in a society where acceptance from others is paramount. But as a self-dependent person you already know that acceptance from others means nothing and changes nothing if we are not accepting of ourselves. Once we accept that it is what it is we can think about it from a different point of view. We can change our thinking from negative to positive. With this change, we can see ourselves and life from an entirely different perspective: one that is positive and happy.

Acceptance that it is what it is takes the fight out of life and frees you up to experience real happiness from the inside out. Let's move on to the next chapter to get some insight about how this concept actually works.

# Happy, Happy, Happy!

N umerous studies show that people who experience real happiness from the inside out see the good in everyone and everything. They are able to see it because they see the good in themselves. Their perception of themselves has shifted from bad to good. As a result, their perception of others follows suit. They not only have high self-regard, they have high regard for others too. They have high other-regard.

### EXPLORATION AND DISCOVERY:

Take an inventory of what is good in your life and society in general. List all that is good. Practice giving your attention to the good in yourself, your life, and society. Pay attention to how much good you are able to see.

People who experience real happiness from the inside out don't need anyone or anything to make them happy. Their happiness is self-dependent. They think themselves into feeling happy. Do you remember the positive thinking-feeling-doing loop from chapter twenty-nine? Let's have some fun and make it a happy thinking-feeling-doing loop. Begin with one happy thought. This one happy thought will kindle a happy feeling, and the happy feeling will ignite happy behaviors. Acting happy prompts more happy thoughts which generate more happy feelings and actuate more happy behaviors, and the happiness thinking-feeling-doing loop continues on without end.

### EXPLORATION AND DISCOVERY:

In chapter fifteen you wrote down your definition of happiness as it was for you at that time. Go back and take a look at it. Has your definition of happiness changed? If so, how do you define happiness now? What has changed? You also made a list of what it took for you to experience "a state of well-being and contentment; a pleasurable and satisfying experience." Make a new list based upon what you are experiencing right now. How does your new list compare to your prior list? Are you happy from the inside out?

Those who experience real happiness from the inside out do not limit themselves to a small life inside their box. They explore the vastness of life in a big world. They make everything, large or small, an adventure. And they do whatever it takes to maintain their happiness from the inside out.

How? Self-dependent people know it's healthy to allow themselves to be supported by others when making major life changes. This might be a good time for a coach. A good coach can provide support, guidance, ideas, and expertise as you pursue your positive thinking. A good coach can often provide information that you didn't know you didn't know about the adventure of life in a big world. Just be sure to remember that it is you who must motivate yourself to embark on the journey. While a good coach can be a great guide, all motivation to complete the exploration is self-motivation.

Because self-dependent people are Good With Me, they no longer require themselves to know everything about everything; they now approve of themselves just the way they are.

Go to www.goodwithme.com/resources for an informative bonus article to learn more about the concept of what you don't know you don't know.

Individuals who enjoy self-dependent esteem do not isolate themselves from others when they aren't on top of their game. They know that it doesn't matter what someone else thinks about them. They realize that what they think about themselves is what really matters.

Those who are self-dependent also enjoy a sense of connectedness to the universe and everything in it. They enjoy connecting with others because they no longer need the approval of others. Support from others keeps them connected and is viewed as a vital component of being a Good With Me person.

From this moment forward, whenever you begin to regress, perhaps returning to negative thoughts, feelings, and behaviors, reach out! Ask for help. Contrary to your other-dependent thinking, this is not a sign of weakness. The ability to recognize the need for support and reaching out for it is a sign of strength! A Good With Me person asks for help when they need it.

Go to the www.goodwithme.com/resources website for great support. Help is just a click away, and it's available 24/7!

## EXPLORATION AND DISCOVERY:

When feeling all alone, unsettled, or like you're losing ground, get out in the world. Even if it's just taking a walk in the park or sitting outside in the grass, you'll gain a sense of connectedness with the rest of the outside world.

If you stumble, remember it's not a failure or a loss. Ted Turner, the founder of Cable News Network (CNN), is an excellent example of never failing. When responding to an interviewer's query about his many Cup of America losses, he said, "I wasn't losing. I was learning how to win." You are not failing during a stumble. You are learning how to move forward. You are learning how to be Good With Me.

In the next chapter you'll learn how to cheer yourself on to the finish line, which is the beginning of your Good With Me journey.

# Go Me!

Go you! Sit or stand on the top of your box and check out the view! Enjoy the new you NOW! Be Good With Me NOW!

Join those who are already on top of their boxes. Join my client Tammy who says, "I can actually say that I have come a long way. At the beginning I used to worry about what everybody thought about me, and now today I have learned it's not all about other people's thoughts, and that I am a strong person. And I'm not afraid. And most of all fear of failing has hindered my progress tremendously. By sticking with this program it has shown me that I can do things I never thought I could do."

Or another client, Rich, who says, "The difference now in what I think about me is now I care. I have goals and believe in myself. In the past I didn't think, care about, or respect myself. Now I enjoy life, and things are going to be the best they've ever been. I really believe that."

A website (www.goodwithme.com/resources) has been designed to assist you in connecting with likeminded individuals. Visit it often to enjoy a sense of connectedness in the universe. It is a place you can go to for peer support every hour of the day, seven days a week. In addition, the website is designed to give you feedback as you complete your *Exploration and Discovery* assignments. This valuable resource is designed to support you as you reinvent who you are and become the person you really want to be. It can even help you change your life story.

> *You are not the events in your life it is how you view them.*
> *You have a chance to reinvent yourself every day.*
> —**Vanessa Williams**, CNN, May 7, 2012

A client, Dick, is someone who has reinvented himself, and he says, "I feel one of the most important things I've learned is that I have a right to feel good about myself. I now continue to pay attention to my own needs and wants and have made it a priority to take good care of myself. As I have been working on my self-esteem, I have noticed that I feel better more and more often, that I am enjoying my life more than I did before, and that I am doing more of the things I have always wanted to do."

To reinvent who you are and to be other-dependent at the same time defeats the purpose. There can be no real happiness from the inside out in that. Conversely, you can now "reinvent" yourself as a person who has self-dependent esteem, who thinks positive thoughts about yourself and life, who no longer allows anyone or anything to spoil your good mood or ruin your day. You can reinvent yourself as someone who is no longer a victim of the words, actions, or opinions of others. You can reinvent yourself to respect your own opinions instead of worrying about what everyone else thinks and dare to be who you are because you are Good With Me! You can now reinvent yourself as someone who knows he or she looks good but doesn't need to look good to be okay. You can now reinvent yourself as someone who likes to be right but doesn't have to be right to be good enough. You can now reinvent yourself as someone who would like to have things turn out the way you want but goes with the flow if they don't. You now know that something good comes out of everything. You now know it's all in the way you think about it.

To reinvent who you are and to be self-dependent is where real happiness from the inside out exists. This is your time to reinvent yourself as someone who is worthy and valued. Reinvent yourself to be the person you always have been but didn't know it. Reinvent yourself to be real. It's easy to be with people who are real. You don't have to prove yourself to anyone anymore. It's okay to be you because you're Good With Me!

**EXPLORATION AND DISCOVERY:**
In chapter six you made some notes about why you complied with what you were expected to do or be by others even though it wasn't what you wanted to do or be.  Go back and review your notes.  Based upon what you have learned, how do you feel now about complying with the expectations of others?  Are you able to reinvent yourself to do and be what you want without worry about the opinions of others or the loss of their approval?

Albert Einstein once said, "Imagination is more important than knowledge. For knowledge is limited to all we now know and understand, while imagination embraces the entire world, and all there ever will be to know and understand." Now you can combine imagination with the knowledge you've gained from your Good With Me experience to be who and what you want to be.

Imagination is very important when reinventing who you are, so let it run wild. Who or what would you be in your wildest, most uninhibited dreams? It's time to become that which you have always wanted to be (as long as it is moral and legal) and heretofore thought was impossible.

You now understand that it was your other-dependent thinking that made your dream seem impossible. Now you know "what a difference a thought makes." Stop allowing your thoughts to limit you. Stop giving up on yourself and giving up your personal identity without giving it a single conscious thought. Stay on top of your box!

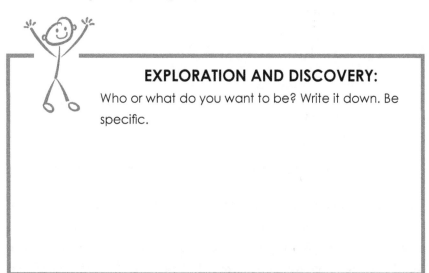

**EXPLORATION AND DISCOVERY:**
Who or what do you want to be? Write it down. Be specific.

Remember this: when you are self-dependent and Good With Me you are happy with yourself just because. You can then be and do whatever you want, or be and do nothing at all, and you will be happy either way because you are no longer other-dependent. Bestselling author W. Clement Stone says that "Whatever the mind of man can conceive and believe, it can achieve." Henry Ford prompted us to remember that "If you think you can do it or you think you can't do it, you are right." So if you think you can, you can.

Become the Little Engine That Could. Make "I think I can, I think I can, I think I can" your permanent lifetime mantra.

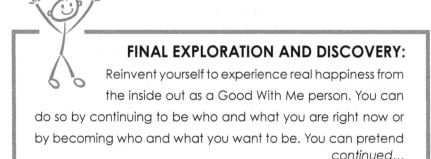

**FINAL EXPLORATION AND DISCOVERY:**
Reinvent yourself to experience real happiness from the inside out as a Good With Me person. You can do so by continuing to be who and what you are right now or by becoming who and what you want to be. You can pretend
*continued...*

*...continued from previous page*
if necessary until it becomes real for you. Keep a journal to chronicle your reinvented self who experiences real happiness from the inside out from high atop your box.

Chinese philosopher Lao-tzu (604-531 BC) taught us that "A journey of a thousand miles begins with a single step." You have already taken a single step. Continue the journey you have begun. Don't wait until later when you have more time to reinvent yourself. Don't put the next step of your life on hold. Don't wait until the next book is written or the next seminar is scheduled. Join my client Brandon, who plans to "continue on the path I'm on and focus on being happy, not finding things to make me happy." Be Good With Me now!

Steve Jobs, the late CEO of Apple Inc, has been quoted as stating, "Simple can be harder than complex: You have to work hard to get your thinking clean to make it simple. But it's worth it in the end because once you get there, you can move mountains." This is exemplified in the following poem by John P. Collins:

Why do I try to impress? When the reality is
It's irrelevant to my success.

If I focus on myself, my goals, and my dreams,
Around the corner I'll find what before was unseen.

In a world where people judge only on what they see,
I must remain focused on what impresses me.

The mind is a powerful thing, keep it opened, let it explore
And you'll see all opportunities that once were ignored.

I once was lost in a world of soul confusion, where
Happiness and love were mental illusions.

I was locked in a basement letting no one inside, feeling
Sorry for myself and losing my pride.

With the help of one I open my eyes and I see all the
things that once were disguised.

*(This poem was inspired by Dr. Patricia Noll. Keeping an open mind and embracing her teachings has helped me to open my eyes and realize that there's more to life than what we see especially when we're under the influence of drugs and alcohol. Clear your mind and experience the high of life itself. —JPC)*

Simple doesn't always mean easy, especially in the beginning when you still think it's hard. It's kind of like taking your first step. It wasn't easy and took a lot of focus and determination. Then it took your commitment to get back up after falling down. But before you knew it you were walking and running. Both became simple and easy to do. It became an automatic behavior that didn't require much thought. You moved the mountain!

You have already taken your first step toward being Good With Me by getting your thinking clean and creating a new reality for yourself through focus, determination, and commitment. Thought establishes your reality, so think yourself into a reality that works. One in which you are self-dependent for your real happiness from the inside out. Create a reality in which you can depend upon you to be Good With Me.

*Good With Me: A Simple Approach to Real Happiness from the Inside Out* ends here, but this is not the end. It is only THE BEGINNING!

# Good With Me
# Resources

I'd love to hear from you! Contact me at www.goodwithme.com to become involved in the Good With Me movement for corporate sponsorships, school programs, speaking engagements, and personal consultations.

I look forward to hearing from you one day soon at www.goodwithme.com/resources.

There might be times when you don't know exactly what to do with a particular assignment. If that happens, just do something. There is no right or wrong way to complete it. A website has been created to assist you with your *Exploration and Discovery* assignments and give you feedback. You can go to www.goodwithme.com/explorationanddiscovery to receive guidance. At this same link you will find the following free articles:

"Comparanoia Slaves"

"Looking Good on Facebook"

"The Bully and the Bullied"

"The Story of You: It's All in Your Head"

"Problem vs. Stuff"

"Don't Give All Your Water Away"

"What You Don't Know You Don't Know"

The website www.goodwithme.com/resources is also designed to help you connect with likeminded individuals. Visit it often to enjoy a sense of connectedness in the universe. It is a place you can go to for peer support every hour of the day, seven days a week. This valuable resource is designed to support you as you reinvent who you are and become the person you really want to be. It can even help you change your life story.

Corporations and private individuals who wish to become Good With Me sponsors may contact Patricia Noll at www.goodwithme.com or www.patricianoll.com for details.

# Exploration and Discovery Index

## Chapter One: So You Want to Be Happy

***Exploration and Discovery***: What do you want to gain from this book? That's right. What do you want to get out of it? What is your reason for picking it up in the first place? Write it down or make a list so you don't lose focus of your purpose.

## Chapter Two: The Two Esteems

***Exploration and Discovery***: Is your self-esteem dependent upon something outside of yourself? If so, what is it? Make a list.

***Exploration and Discovery***: What is your idea of self-esteem right now? Write it down so you can compare it with any changes that occur in your idea of self-esteem as you move forward.

## Chapter Three: Self-Dependent Esteem

***Exploration and Discovery***: Do you consider yourself a person of worth and value just because you exist? Or is your value and worth other-dependent with all sorts of conditions attached to it? If so make a list of the conditions attached to your worth and value. Is your self-confidence dependent upon external criteria? If so make a list of the external criteria.

*Exploration and Discovery:* Do you have self-dependent esteem? What makes you think you have it? This assignment is a catch-22 because in a sense you have to have some level of self-dependent esteem to admit you don't have it. If your esteem was fully other dependent, you would have a hard time admitting to anyone—including yourself—that you may not have it all together. With that in mind, be honest with yourself and admit that you don't have self-dependent esteem if that is true for you. See if you can identify the external criteria that are the source of your esteem.

*Exploration and Discovery:* Do you want to have self-dependent esteem? What do you think will be different when you have it? How will you know when you have it?

## Chapter Four: Other-Dependent Esteem

*Exploration and Discovery:* What type of esteem do you think you have? Is it self-dependent or other-dependent? Does any esteem you have for yourself depend upon the approval of others? How much of knowing you look good is based upon external criteria?

*Exploration and Discovery:* How do you feel about yourself when you experience a glitch in the way your life is turning out or when something you depended upon to feel good about yourself no longer exists?

*Exploration and Discovery:* What if you never receive another compliment from anyone? How do you think you would feel about yourself?

## Chapter Five: The Four Attachments

*Exploration and Discovery:* Do you identify with any of the Four Attachments at this time? If so, which ones and in what ways? Make a list.

## Chapter Six: Attachment # 1:
## The Need for Approval from Others

*Exploration and Discovery:* Before going any further, see if you can identify what you think others think about you. Make some notes to revisit at a later time.

*Exploration and Discovery:* How important is approval from others to you? How much do you depend upon it to tell you if you are good enough—or not?

*Exploration and Discovery*: How important are the opinions of others about you? Do you allow other people's opinions of you to determine the choices you make? Whose opinions do you value more than your own? Have you let them influence the career you pursued, the kind of house you live in, the car you drive, or the people you choose for friends? Do you let the opinions of others affect what you wear or even what you eat? Make a list.

*Exploration and Discovery*: What is the price you pay for needing approval from others? Make a list.

*Exploration and Discovery*: How often do you say yes when you really want to say no? Make a list. Do you resent others for asking?

*Exploration and Discovery*: What were you expected to do or be that you didn't want for yourself? Did you comply? If so, why did you comply? Make some notes to review later on.

*Exploration and Discovery*: Make a list of what you *do* want. Every time you think of something you do want, add it to the list.

*Exploration and Discovery*: How have you contradicted your values and morals just to make sure someone, especially your chosen peer group, has a good opinion of you? What were the results of your choice to do so?

*Exploration and Discovery*: If you have given up and don't care what others think about you, be honest with yourself. Is it because you have esteem for yourself, or is it a roundabout way for you to "wow" others into having a good opinion of you?

*Exploration and Discovery*: Do you relate to this example? If so, in what way?

## Chapter Seven: Attachment # 2: The Need to Look Good

*Exploration and Discovery*: What does looking good mean to you? What have you done in the past to look good? What are you doing right now to look good? Make a list.

*Exploration and Discovery*: How much do you allow the media to influence your definition of looking good? Make a list.

*Exploration and Discovery*: What about yourself do you compare to others? Do you compare your education to theirs? Do you compare your dysfunctional family to their well-adjusted family? Do you compare your nose to hers? Do you compare your thinning hair to his thick hair? Do you compare yourself to the "beautiful people" or the "important people" who appear on the covers of magazines? Make a list for yourself.

*Exploration and Discovery:* How much of yourself do you deny or try to hide from others to look good and appear to be right?

## Chapter Eight: Attachment #3: The Need to Be Right

*Exploration and Discovery:* Are you a know-it-all? How important is it to be seen as someone who knows what you're talking about or what you're doing? Or to be seen as someone who knows it all?

*Exploration and Discovery:* How important is it for you to be right? How have you behaved just to prove a point?

*Exploration and Discovery:* How do you feel about being wrong? How do you react when you are wrong?

## Chapter Nine: Attachment #4: The Need to Control the Outcome

*Exploration and Discovery:* How important is it to you that everything turns out the way you think it should? Are you someone who worries about the way situations may or may not turn out? Does everything in its entirety need to turn out the way you think it should? Are you overly concerned with outcomes or results?

*Exploration and Discovery:* What do you do to get everything to turn out the way you think it should and get your own way? Be brutally honest with yourself on this one! You may never have paid any attention to how unacceptable and inappropriate your behavior is. Realize that your lack of self-dependent esteem and your need for other-dependent esteem can make it nearly impossible for you to identify your unacceptable and inappropriate choice of behaviors. Do the best you can with it. Remember: the more honest you are with yourself, the greater the progress will be toward becoming a Good With Me person.

*Exploration and Discovery:* How do you try to control people, places, and/or things? Are you a "control freak"? Do you manipulate? Are you an instigator? Are you the one who needles others with sarcasm to accomplish your goal? Do you goad others into following you? Do you intimidate others into succumbing to your direction?

*Exploration and Discovery*: What do you do when others don't choose to do what you want them to do? What attempts have you made to control the uncontrollable? Make a list.

## Chapter Ten: Thinking Makes It So

*Exploration and Discovery*: Recall a time when you thought a certain way about something and later changed your mind about it. Did you think you were right before you changed your mind? Did you also think you were right after you changed your mind? Which part of your thinking was actually right—before you changed your mind or after? Are you beginning to realize that changing your thinking changed your reality?

*Exploration and Discovery*: Can you remember a time when you thought someone was downright awful? All the while you knew you were "dead right" about him or her until something changed your mind at a later time. What was responsible for your change in attitude toward that person? Which thought was accurate? Do you remember how you might have been thinking about yourself before and after you changed your mind?

*Exploration and Discovery*: Begin to pay attention to the thoughts you have about yourself. What kind of thoughts are you thinking about you? Make a list. Now challenge your list by determining if your thoughts are accurate or inaccurate. What kind of proof do you have that your thoughts are accurate or inaccurate?

*Exploration and Discovery*: Pay attention to your thinking for a day. Keep a log of your thoughts throughout the day. See if you can notice what kind of thoughts you are having. Can you tell if they are positive or negative? You will have to remind yourself continually to be conscious of your thinking. This will take lots of energy, so don't become discouraged when some of your thoughts get past you unnoticed. You, like almost everyone else, may have spent a lifetime ignoring your thoughts.

*Exploration and Discovery*: Sit down and think about how good you are. Repeat this throughout this day and every day for the remainder of your life. Can't think of anything good about you? If not, then make something up and think about it over and over again throughout the day. Don't mistake this for encouraging untrue and delusional thinking. There is something good about every single one of us. Sometimes we just have to find it—and beginning with something made-up may lead you to the truth about the good in you. You could even ask a friend or family member to point out something good about you and think about it throughout the day. Or find a word in the dictionary that describes a good trait or characteristic in you that you had forgotten you had and make it your mantra for the day. Then find a new word to describe a good trait or characteristic about yourself each and every day.

## Chapter Eleven: So You Think?

***Exploration and Discovery***: Take ownership of the way you think and feel about yourself. Wake up from your auto-pilot thinking and begin to monitor the way you think about you. What kind of thoughts do you think about yourself? What is the driving force behind them? It can be hard at first to identify a thought. If this is the case for you, the way you feel is your clue to the thought you are thinking. Your feelings can help you identify the thoughts that led to them. Identify the way you feel about yourself first. Once you identify the way you feel, ask yourself what you were thinking to create this feeling.

## Chapter Twelve: Sick with Worry

***Exploration and Discovery***: So who do you think is worried about starting the new job and who isn't? See if you can make the distinction between the worrier and the non-worrier. Remember it is the same job position, same rate of pay, same hours, same everything for every one of them.

***Exploration and Discovery***: Which of the above examples do you identify with? Are you able to see that it is your thinking and not the situation that creates your worry? Write about it.

***Exploration and Discovery***: Recall things you have worried about in the past that never happened. Compare what you worried about to what actually happened. Did you expend a lot of energy being worried for nothing?

***Exploration and Discovery***: To eliminate worry, you have to change your thoughts about a situation or person. Instead of thinking about a dreaded outcome, think about the countless ways it could turn out great or at the very least okay. If at first you come up blank with a positive outcome, think about one single thing in life you are grateful for. This is a distraction tactic. Once you have distracted yourself from thinking about a dreaded outcome, the next step is to think about how you would like the circumstance to turn out. Just a single thought is good enough. It might not be easy at first, but you can do it. Remain conscious of your thinking, and whenever you notice yourself having a worrisome thought, think once again about a positive outcome.

## Chapter Thirteen: My Stress Is Killing Me!

*Exploration and Discovery:* What stresses you? Make a list.

*Exploration and Discovery*: What are you doing or what have you done to manage your stress or to rid yourself of stress?

*Exploration and Discovery*: Think once again about the things that cause you stress. For example, responsibilities, paying the bills, the bank balance, the job, the boss, a relationship breakup, physical health, a medical diagnosis, deadlines, a fast-paced lifestyle, or even the trauma of war. A common cause of stress for many women is juggling a job/career, her husband and kids, and her home. Similarly, many who are the head of a family are stressed over being good providers. What are the causes of your stress as you see them now? Write them down.

*Exploration and Discovery*: Allow yourself to be open to the idea that feeling stressed-out means you are thinking stressful thoughts, and that stress is nothing more or nothing less than that. Pay specific attention to the thoughts you are having each and every time you feel stressed. See if you can identify the thought you had that preceded the feeling of stress. The more you pay attention to what you are thinking, the easier it will be to see that the way you think is responsible for your stress. After all, if there actually was an inherently stressful situation or person, everyone who encounters it would have to be stressed by it. Put it to the test for yourself with the following example.

*Exploration and Discovery*: Notice your thoughts and see if you can change the way you are thinking about whatever it is that is stressing you out. This might not be easy at first, and changing the way you think about some situations will be easier than others. As an example, you may be stressing over getting to work on time, so you might change your thinking to *Relax. It is what it is. Everything is going to be okay. Being stressed won't get me there any sooner.* This is not to make you believe it is okay to be late but to realize that being stressed will not change the outcome. When you succeed at changing your thoughts, the feeling of stress will begin to disappear.

*Exploration and Discovery*: Why do you stress? Is it a way to get approval or to fit in and belong? How often do you one-up your friends or coworkers with your stress?

*Exploration and Discovery*: Show another that you care deeply without being stressed. What is your experience?

*Exploration and Discovery*: Pay attention to the thoughts you are having about the day. Are they good or bad? Are they stress-producing? If they are good, create more of them. If they are bad, think about one thing that is good about your day. Perhaps it is as simple as waking up this morning. Maybe it is that you have air to breathe or water to drink. You get the idea. Dig deep if necessary to find something good. Even though it might not be easy at first, think about your good instead of your bad. When you notice yourself thinking about what's bad, consciously shift your thinking to what's good. Do this as many times as need be until you are having more thoughts about your good than about your bad. It will become easier with each time you make the shift from bad to good.

## Chapter Fourteen: Don't Manage the Damage

*Exploration and Discovery*: Practice changing negative stress-producing thoughts into positive, calming thoughts. Pick a situation in which you would normally become stressed. Identify the type of thoughts you would normally have in that situation. Can you identify the stress-producing thoughts? Once you have identified the stress-producing thoughts, change them to positive, calming thoughts. Create your own personal positive, calming words for this situation and then repeat them over and over again. This is likely to feel strange, even uncomfortable at first, because you are used to feeling stressed out. You might not even believe it is possible to change your stress-producing thoughts to positive, calming thoughts. If and when this happens, just notice that you are uncomfortable and keep on thinking positive, calming thoughts about the situation. Speak the words out loud.

Continue this process until you are able to get past your discomfort and your own negative stress-producing thoughts.

## Chapter Fifteen: The Two Happys

*Exploration and Discovery*: What were you taught about what it takes to be happy in life? Write it down. Were you told you have to have the right friends (including which ones were right and which ones weren't)? Did you have to find the right relationship partner? How important was it to fit in and belong with the right group of people? Was it expected that you would be popular within your peer group? What about getting good grades in school, the right education, the right degree from the right college or university, graduating with honors, and finally choosing the right career? What about being good in athletics, band, cheerleading? What about wearing the right clothes, especially the right designer labels? What about driving the right automobile, or residing in the perfect house in the best neighborhood? Make a list of what you have considered to be the "right stuff" to make you happy. And don't be surprised if it's a long list.

*Exploration and Discovery:* What is your definition of happiness? Remember, it can be whatever it is for you right now. Write it down and save it for later.

*Exploration and Discovery*: What does it take for you to experience "a state of well-being and contentment; a pleasurable and satisfying experience?" Do you even know? Make your list and save it for later.

*Exploration and Discovery*: Are you thinking yourself into being happy? Are you someone who is happy "just because"? Or are you someone who has decided that being happy is just too hard?

*Exploration and Discovery*: Which of the above do you identify with? Make a list and note how each one of the negative effects usually leads to more unhappiness.

## Chapter Sixteen: Unhappiness:
## The Price of Other-Dependent Needs

*Exploration and Discovery:* Take a look at your own other-dependent needs, i.e. the need for approval from others, looking good to others, being right, and the need to control the outcome, among others. Describe the severity of each. Compile a list of consequences you have experienced due to your other-dependent needs. Include the negative effects of each one. Do your best to look at every area of your life. Especially notice if the price of your other-dependent needs is a greater degree of unhappiness. Notice if your unhappiness has simply become normal for you. Are you trapped in a catch-22 of other-dependent needs that lead to more unhappiness, and unhappiness that leads to more other-dependent needs?

## Chapter Seventeen: I Don't Have an Addiction, Do I?

*Exploration and Discovery*: What have you used to cope with life to feel better or at least to feel less bad? Make a list. Do you have a favorite? What is it?

*Exploration and Discovery*: How has the addictive use of your favored coping mechanism diminished your quality of life? Make a list.

## Chapter Eighteen: What's My Problem?

*Exploration and Discovery:* Make a list of some of the negative, bad, or uncomfortable feelings you have tried to fix by depending upon someone or something outside of yourself.

*Exploration and Discovery*: Look at your list of negative, bad, or uncomfortable feelings you have attempted to change. Now make a list of the people, places, or things you have depended upon to make you feel better. What was the result of each? Did they work or not? What additional problems were created by them?

## Chapter Nineteen: The Escape Artists

*Exploration and Discovery*: What poor and perhaps self-destructive choices have you made to escape feeling bad? For example, when did you eat a whole bag of chips while watching your favorite television program, or spend part of the rent money to buy something you just had to have, or downed too many drinks even though you had plans with family or friends? How about being flirtatious with the boss or a coworker for attention, compromising your safety or reputation just to be a part of the group, or even yelling in front of everyone just to make a point? Make a list.

*Exploration and Discovery*: Have you thought of any other escape mechanisms you use that seem socially acceptable? How do you justify your escape mechanism of choice?

*Exploration and Discovery*: Give yourself permission to have real fun. You may choose to do something you think is fun, playful, or even frivolous. Or you may choose to think yourself into having fun while doing nothing at all. Remember, thinking makes it so. You may not utilize whatever you have done in the past to escape. Write about your experience. If you don't have fun doing what you have chosen to do, you don't have to do it again, but you won't know if it is fun or not until you do it.

## Chapter Twenty: The New Normal

*Exploration and Discovery*: What abnormal behaviors have you normalized for yourself without realizing it? How do you minimize, rationalize, and justify engaging in them to others? How do you minimize, rationalize, and justify engaging in them to yourself?

*Exploration and Discovery*: What are the results and/or consequences of your own new-normal behaviors? Make a list.

*Exploration and Discovery*: Make a list of the new-normal activities you engage in and your motive for doing them. What are your reasons for doing what you do? Are you able to recognize your other-dependency? Do you recognize your attempt to make yourself happy?

*Exploration and Discovery*: Do your best to identify the abnormal behaviors you have normalized in your pursuit of real happiness. You may not have realized prior to right now that you were engaging in these abnormal behaviors just to make yourself feel good. Once again, see if you can recognize why you have been engaging in these abnormal behaviors. What was your motive? Was it instant gratification? For clarity, these abnormal behaviors do not include an occasional fast-food meal or the moderate use of Facebook.

## Chapter Twenty-One: The Feel-Good-Now Syndrome

*Exploration and Discovery*: What can't you do without? What do you need to make yourself feel good now? Make a list.

*Exploration and Discovery*: If you experience emotional or physical pain, I want you to focus on anything and everything you currently have to be grateful for. Perhaps someone special who provides love and care for you, a good neighbor, a pet, a bed to sleep in, food to eat, a good book to read, a favorite television show to watch, a rainy day, a sunny day, the fact that you are alive. Nothing is too big or too small to put on your list. Start making your list now.

## Chapter Twenty-Two: The Great Pretenders

*Exploration and Discovery*: Is there anything you are trying to hide about yourself? Can you identify any of your secrets? Write them all down—don't leave any out. What are you afraid of? What do you fear other people might find out about you? Be brutally honest with yourself as you make your list.

*Exploration and Discovery*: What have you done to try to keep your secret a secret? How much energy has it taken to do so? How bad are the negative effects of trying to hide it?

## Chapter Twenty-Three: Different Just Like You

*Exploration and Discovery*: Have you ever admired a particular person or group of people who were different and chose to be different just like them? See if you can identify who that was. What were the results?

*Exploration and Discovery*: How important is it to you to be different just like your chosen group? Do you feel something is wrong with you because you are different from others? How are you different from others? What are the good points about being different from others? Write about it.

*Exploration and Discovery*: Can you add some of your own ideas and societal conditioning to this list? Write them down here.

*Exploration and Discovery*: Do you need to be more and have more than others to convince yourself that you are better than others? Do you believe that "your kind of different" makes you better than others?

## Chapter Twenty-Four: Get in Where You Fit In

*Exploration and Discovery*: What have you been willing to risk just to fit in and belong? What price have you been willing to pay in order to fit in and belong?

*Exploration and Discovery*: What have you jeopardized in order to fit in and belong? What consequences have you experienced due to your choice to do whatever it takes to fit in and belong? Write about it.

*Exploration and Discovery*: Make a list of the choices you made as a teenager to fit in and belong. The following narrative may be helpful to you in figuring this out for yourself.

*Exploration and Discovery*: Now that you've made a list of what you did to fit in and belong as a teenager, think about how you felt about yourself when you took those actions, then describe your feelings. How many of them are still important to you now?

*Exploration and Discovery*: See if you can identify some of the less obvious ways you tried to fit in and belong. Make a list.

## Chapter Twenty-Five: It's All About Me

*Exploration and Discovery*: I am sure you remember most of your significant performances. How often have you *performed* for your audience because you thought that all eyes were on you? Who were they for? What was each performance like? Write about them.

*Exploration and Discovery*: You already have a mental list about the way you think others scrutinize you. Write it down.

*Exploration and Discovery*: What do you think others think about you? Do you personalize what you think others think about you? See if you can remember a time or two when you personalized what you thought someone else was thinking about you. How do you know what they were thinking about you? You made some notes in chapter six to revisit at a later time. They were about identifying what you think others think about you. Let's revisit your notes now. How do they compare to what you think now about what others think about you? Has your thinking about what others think about you changed? If so, in what way has it changed?

*Exploration and Discovery*: Do you personalize what others say about you or how they treat you? Do you ever make up your own version of what you think their opinion is about you and believe it?

*Exploration and Discovery*: How much importance do you place upon what *you* think about yourself?

## Chapter Twenty-Six: What a Difference a Thought Makes

***Exploration and Discovery***: Notice that you are having thoughts all the time. Those thoughts are not only creating your experience of life, they are creating the way you experience yourself. Especially notice if any of your thoughts are putting you down or making you doubt your ability to create a life experience that includes real happiness from the inside out. Are they saying something like: *This isn't going to work for me* or *I'm not going to be able to do this*? If so, you have to change your thoughts about yourself and what you are capable of achieving. See if you can change them now. What is the outcome?

***Exploration and Discovery***: Think yourself into feeling good. Begin by closing your eyes. Take a deep breath and notice what you are thinking. Just notice whatever it is without making it right or wrong. Then begin thinking about a time when something extra-good happened to you. Think about how good you felt at the time. If you can't think of anything extra-good that has happened to you, you can imagine a "what if" of something extra-good that you would like to experience. Notice how you begin to feel good right now for no particular reason other than that you are thinking about a wonderful time in your life. If and when the negative chatter starts to interfere with your good time, just shift your thoughts back to your good experience. The negative chatter will not give up without a fight. It has been running the show for a long time and is now a habit. So you'll have to remain conscious of your thoughts to shift them to a happy time in your life whenever the negative chatter tries to creep in and ruin your positive thinking experience. Each time you shift from your negative chatter to your good experience is proof that you can do this. Now you know that you can think yourself into feeling good. Now you know what a difference a thought makes.

***Exploration and Discovery***: Create your own "thinking yourself into feeling happy right now" mantra. Use it as your new positive message default. Repeat it over and over throughout the day. Notice how happy you feel when you do so. You are experiencing real happiness from the inside out, perhaps for the first time.

## Chapter Twenty-Seven: Celebrate Me!

*Exploration and Discovery*: Think one single positive thought about yourself. I'm sure you can come up with one by now. But if you can't come up with one positive thought about yourself, make one up for now. You could also imagine a "what if" positive thought about yourself that you would like to have, or you can ask a close friend or family member to tell you about a quality they see in you that you don't see in yourself. Or pick one from the list that follows:

- I like the color of my eyes.
- I have healthy legs.
- I have strong toes.
- I am kind.
- I am a good friend.
- I love nature.
- I am a good worker.
- I am a survivor.

Now keep repeating your positive thought over and over throughout the day. What happens? Write about it.

*Exploration and Discovery:* Speak directly to your negative thoughts when they occur. Have a list ready to combat them before they even happen. Your list can consist of something like this:

- Go away.
- You don't have a home here anymore.
- I'm over you.
- You don't know what you're talking about.
- I'm done with you.
- You make me laugh.
- I don't believe you anymore.
- You're toast.
- You don't own me anymore.

Now make up some of your own. Write them down to use whenever a negative thought pops into your mind. It's always good to have several methods to overcome negative thoughts.

## Chapter Twenty-Eight: Positive-Up!

*Exploration and Discovery*: Make a list of your self-perceived uncontrollable character defects or personality flaws.

*Exploration and Discovery*: Create your own personal ceremony to destroy the list you just made. For example, you can shred it, bury it, or burn it safely in a bowl. Whatever your personal ceremony, be sure it symbolically destroys any residual thinking you may have about your self-perceived character defects and personality flaws.

*Exploration and Discovery*: Make a list of all the positive qualities about you. Have fun with this. You can even use your imagination and list the qualities you *want* to be true about you. Relish them. Place them on sticky notes everywhere—on your bathroom mirror, on your mobile phone, on the steering wheel of your car, on your desk, in your office cubicle, and any other location where you will see them often. Make sure you look at them often. Speak them out loud so that your own ears can hear them. This is the new you!

## Chapter Twenty-Nine: Practice Makes Better

*Exploration and Discovery*: Can you think of any negative behaviors you've engaged in over and over just to make yourself feel better? Make a list. Can you recognize any of the repetitive negative thoughts you have had about yourself as a result of your habitual negative behaviors? Make a list. Did it ever occur to you that you are very good at resorting to these negative behaviors and thoughts because practice makes better?

*Exploration and Discovery*: Practice esteeming who you are. Make a list of words that are self-esteeming. These words begin with "self."

- Self-prideful
- Self-admiring
- Self-approving
- Self-confident

- Self-important
- Self-loving
- Self-respecting
- Self-satisfied

Add your own self-esteeming words to this list. Notice that these words are about you esteeming yourself and have nothing to do with the way others esteem you. They have nothing to do with approval from others, looking good to others, being right, or controlling the way others think about you. They have nothing to do with your material possessions, education, knowledge, accomplishments, friends, or money in the bank. They exist within you just because you exist and not because of what you have, do, or know. They are an expression of you just because you are you. Be sure to make the practice of esteeming yourself a fun experience.

Utilize the positive thinking-feeling-doing loop as you practice esteeming yourself. The loop works like this. You think a self-esteeming word about yourself, which leads to feeling esteem for who you are. When you feel esteem for who you are your behavior will reflect the esteem you have for you. For example, the more you esteem who you are the easier it is for you to see yourself with softer and kinder eyes; you begin to see past what you have, do, and know. Your reaction to this will be holding your head high with self-pride no matter what. This prompts another self-esteeming word that engenders feelings of contentment, satisfaction, and happiness. These feelings foster kindness toward you. Your kindness toward yourself provokes more acceptance of yourself, which you act out in your everyday routine, and the loop continues without end. This is the powerful self-esteeming thinking-feeling-doing loop at work.

## Chapter Thirty: Deliberate Intentional Practice Makes Better Faster

***Exploration and Discovery:*** Practice believing the self-esteeming positive thoughts about yourself with deliberate intention. Focus on your specific goal of esteeming you without depending upon anyone or anything outside of you to give you approval or make you look good. Monitor the way you feel about yourself to know if you are beginning to believe the self-esteeming positive thoughts you are having about yourself. Do you notice a shift in the way you feel? Are you beginning to believe the self-esteeming positive thoughts you are having about you? Are you internalizing them? Are you taking ownership of them and making them yours for real? Take corrective action to shift from uncertainty to belief. Counter every negative thought with a self-esteeming positive thought.

Use your practice list of self-esteeming positive thoughts from chapter 29 to support your corrective action and deepen your belief that you have real value from the inside out.

Begin by paying attention to the thoughts that truly help you esteem yourself from the inside out just because you exist.

- Which ones are easier to believe?
- Which self-esteeming thoughts work best to make you feel good/ happy?
- Notice the thoughts that don't work and eliminate them.
- Repeat the thoughts that make you believe you have value just because you exist over and over with deliberate intention.
- Create a self-esteeming mantra about you by using the thoughts that invoke self-esteem.
- Practice reciting your self-esteeming mantra hour after hour throughout the day with deliberate intention.

Next, pay attention to your thinking patterns.

- Are there times when self-esteeming thoughts are more prevalent?
- Are certain self-esteeming thoughts easier to notice than others?
- Are there times when you resist the idea of thinking something good about yourself?
- Are there times when the need for approval from others is more prevalent?
- Are certain needs for approval from others easier to catch than others?

Now, pay attention to what works and what doesn't work to negate the need for approval from others.

- What works best to turn your self-critical putdowns into positive feedback?
- Do you notice a power struggle between your need for approval from others and your self-esteeming thinking?
- What prohibits you from thinking self-esteem thoughts about yourself?
- What fosters self-esteeming thoughts?
- Give yourself honest and direct feedback about what does and doesn't work.
- Improve upon what worked with deliberate intentional practice.

As you practice with deliberate intention, you will shift your other-dependent esteem to self-dependent esteem in no time. It will occur faster than you might have imagined possible.

*Exploration and Discovery*: Make a list of what you are consciously doing to shift your other-dependent esteem to self-dependent esteem. Make a list of what you are changing to eliminate the need for someone or something outside of yourself to make you happy. Make a list of the various ways you are now able to make yourself happy all by yourself.

## Chapter Thirty-One: Repetition Works

*Exploration and Discovery*: Begin your own personal Good With Me advertising campaign by showering yourself with praise over and over for hours every day. Make a list, a very long list, of complimentary words to repeat to yourself about yourself. Choose at least one complimentary word to repeat each day. Repeat it all day long. Notice how you feel at the end of the day.

## Chapter Thirty-Two: The Measures of Success

*Exploration and Discovery*: Chart your success by paying attention to how good/happy you feel. Notice how much better you feel about yourself with no strings attached.

*Exploration and Discovery*: Notice how much fun it is to keep track of the increase in your positive internal chatter. Notice how much fun it is to measure your success as a positive thinker.

## Chapter Thirty-Three: Word Power

*Exploration and Discovery*: Pay attention to your use of the words *try, can't, but, wish, hope,* and *problem*. For now, make a mental note whenever you think or speak them.

*Exploration and Discovery*: Recall a time when you used the word *try* to avoid doing something you didn't want to do because it allowed you to save face at a later time. Can you recall how you felt?

*Exploration and Discovery*: Use repetitive deliberate intentional practice to say no instead of *I'll try* when a situation calls for doing so. Are you able to stop yourself from saying *I'll try*? Can you say no without justification? Do you still have the need to justify saying no? Do you feel different about yourself when you say no? Write about your results.

*Exploration and Discovery*: Use deliberate intentional practice to avoid using the word *can't* in your speaking. Notice what you feel when you do so, and write about it.

*Exploration and Discovery*: Pay attention to your *wishing* and *hoping* thoughts. Can you see how they are keeping you stuck not only inside of your box, but in your life? Notice how often you utilize these two words.

*Exploration and Discovery:* Use repetitive deliberate intentional practice to replace the word *but* with the word *and*. What do you notice?

*Exploration and Discovery:* Use repetitive deliberate intentional practice to replace the word *problem* with *stuff*. Notice what happens. And be sure to check out the entire article "Problem vs. Stuff" on www.goodwithme.com/resources.

## Chapter Thirty-Four: Me First, You Second

*Exploration and Discovery*: Give yourself permission to put you first and others second. Notice how you think and feel when you first begin to practice healthy selfishness with deliberate intention.

*Exploration and Discovery*: Think about the times when you have resented someone you were helping. Have you ever wondered when it would be your turn to be taken care of? Have you thought or said "After all I've done for you…?" If so, make a list of those times.

*Exploration and Discovery*: Nurture yourself. Do all the things for yourself that you do for others. Do the things for yourself that you want others to do for you.

*Exploration and Discovery*: When someone tells you how selfish you are becoming as you practice healthy selfishness by setting boundaries, respond with a simple "thank you." They don't realize they have actually given you a compliment. Their compliment is proof that your repetitive practice with deliberate intention is working for you. You no longer have to take care of everyone else first so that they like you and have a good opinion of you. Pleasing others is no longer your first priority. You are shifting from other-dependent esteem to self-dependent esteem.

## Chapter Thirty-Five: What Fun It Is!

*Exploration and Discovery*: What kind of child's play would you like to indulge in now that you are no longer afraid you might look foolish to others? Write a short description.

*Exploration and Discovery*: Practice having fun with deliberate intention. Make having fun an adventure. Use your imagination and go on your fun adventure. Write about the results.

*Exploration and Discovery*: Find out how it feels to have fun like a child. Make a list of ways to play. Make a list of anything and everything you think could be fun for you. Then choose one thing from your list and do it within the week. Chart your level of fun.

*Exploration and Discovery*: Think yourself into having fun for no particular reason. Think yourself into having fun walking down a new street, listening to an old song, playing with a baby, preparing a friend's great recipe, volunteering for an event, and anything else you choose to do for no particular reason.

## Chapter Thirty-Six: It Is What It Is

*Exploration and Discovery*: Practice accepting that it is what it is. How do you feel when you do? If you truly accept that "whatever" is what it is, you will notice that any stress you were experiencing begins to diminish. Your whole body will start to relax.

## Chapter Thirty-Seven: Happy, Happy, Happy!

*Exploration and Discovery*: Take an inventory of what is good in your life and society in general. List all that is good. Practice giving your attention to the good in yourself, your life, and society. Pay attention to how much good you are able to see.

*Exploration and Discovery:* In chapter fifteen you wrote down your definition of happiness as it was for you at that time. Go back and take a look at it. Has your definition of happiness changed? If so, how do you define happiness now? What has changed? You also made a list of what it took for you to experience "a state of well-being and contentment; a pleasurable and satisfying experience." Make a new list based upon what you are experiencing right now. How does your new list compare to your prior list? Are you happy from the inside out?

*Exploration and Discovery*: When feeling all alone, unsettled, or like you're losing ground, get out in the world. Even if it's just taking a walk in the park or sitting outside in the grass, you'll gain a sense of connectedness with the rest of the outside world.

## Chapter Thirty-Eight: Go Me!

*Exploration and Discovery*: In chapter six you made some notes about why you complied with what you were expected to do or be by others even though it wasn't what you wanted to do or be. Go back and review your notes. Based upon what you have learned, how do you feel now about complying with the expectations of others? Are you able to reinvent yourself to do and be what you want without worry about the opinions of others or the loss of their approval?

*Exploration and Discovery*: Who or what do you want to be? Write it down. Be specific.

*Final Exploration and Discovery*: Reinvent yourself to experience real happiness from the inside out as a Good With Me person. You can do so by continuing to be who and what you are right now or by becoming who and what you want to be. You can pretend if necessary until it becomes real for you. Keep a journal to chronicle your reinvented self who experiences real happiness from the inside out from high atop your box.

# About the Author

**Patricia Noll** is an author, speaker, and founder of Focus One, Inc., an outpatient substance abuse treatment program that has been licensed by the State of Florida since September 1989.

She has given more than five thousand group lectures and presentations on self-esteem, healthy relationships, and addictive behaviors. She is a CBS affiliate televised industry expert with a master's degree in mental health counseling and a degree in traditional Chinese medicine. Her credentials include:

- Licensed mental health counselor
- Certified addictions professional
- Acupuncture physician
- U.S. Department of Transportation substance abuse professional
- U.S. Nuclear Regulatory Commission substance abuse expert

Patricia combines all of these modalities to create an effective treatment protocol for substance abuse recovery and mental health issues.

As an expert on self-esteem, Patricia specializes in teaching people how to feel good about who they are just because they exist. She has received thousands of client testimonials sharing the dynamic results in their lives. Her mission and passion is to make a difference in the way people see themselves—especially those who have given up on life—by starting a Good With Me™ movement throughout the world.

She invites everyone who wants to feel real happiness from the inside out to join her. Learn how at www.goodwithme.com/movement.

# Notes

1  Center for Disease Control, CNN

2  Ibid.

3  Cass and Holford, *Natural Highs* (2002)

4  Ibid.

5  Deadly Dose with Dr. Sanjay Gupta, CNN

6  *St. Petersburg Times*, July 1, 2009

7  CNN

8  Fareed Zakaria, CNN, December 11, 2011

9  Mr. Shulman, Something for Nothing, Recovery Today, Volume 17, Number 12

10  CNN, April 1, 2012

11  Fareed Zakaria, CNN, June 3, 2012

12  "Incarceration Nation from the High Budgetary Cost of Incarceration"

13  Fareed Zakaria, CNN, April 1, 2012

14  15  The Human Cognition Project, hcp.lumosity.com/research/neuroscience

16  Ibid.

Printed in the USA
CPSIA information can be obtained
at www.ICGtesting.com
JSHW082228140824
68134JS00017B/793